t

Baedeker's
BUDAPEST

Imprint

Cover picture: Fishermen's Bastion

80 colour pictures, 7 plans, 7 ground-plans, 1 graphic representation, 1 transport plan, 1 city plan

Text:
Helmut Linde, Reutlingen
Editorial work:
Baedeker staff

General direction:
Dr Peter Baumgarten, Baedeker Stuttgart

Cartography:
Georg Schiffner, Lahr
Franz Kaiser, Sindelfingen,
Cartographia, Budapest (city plan)

Source of illustrations:
Anthony (1), Handl (12), Historia-Photo (9), IBUSZ (15), IPV (17), Jenninger (1), Linde (17), MDV (2), Oberländer (6)

English translation: Alec Court

Following the tradition established by Karl Baedeker in 1844, sights of particular interest and hotels of particular quality are distinguished by either one or two asterisks.

To make it easier to locate the various sights listed in the "A to Z" section of the guide, their coordinates on the city plan are shown in red at the head of each entry.

Only a selection of hotels and restaurants can be given: no reflection is implied, therefore, on establishments not included.

In a time of rapid change it is difficult to ensure that all the information given is entirely accurate and up to date, and the possibility of error can never be entirely eliminated. Although the publishers can accept no responsibility for inaccuracies and omissions, they are always grateful for corrections and suggestions for improvement.

Contents

Preface

This Pocket Guide to Budapest is one of the new generation of Baedeker city guides.

Baedeker pocket guides, illustrated throughout in colour, are designed to meet the needs of the modern traveller. They are quick and easy to consult, with the principal sights described in alphabetical order and practical details about opening times, how to get there, etc., shown in the margin.

Each guide is divided into three parts. The first part gives a general account of the city, its history, population, culture and so on; in the second part the principal sights are described; and the third part contains a variety of practical information designed to help visitors to find their way about and to make the most of their stay.

The new guides are abundantly illustrated and contain numbers of newly drawn plans. At the back of the book is a large city map, and each entry in the main part of the guide gives the coordinates of the square on the map in which the particular feature can be located. Users of this guide, therefore, will have no difficulty in finding what they want to see.

Facts and Figures

General

Budapest, the capital of the Hungarian People's Republic is considered by many visitors to be the "Paris of the East", because of its particular charm; after Moscow and Leningrad it is the most densely populated and economically and culturally the most important metropolis of Eastern Central Europe. Budapest came into being in 1872 by the amalgamation of three previously independent towns, Obuda (Old Buda), Buda and Pest, and subsequently spread quickly on both sides of the Danube. Thanks to its favourable geographical position this leading political, administrative, industrial and commercial centre of Hungary maintains many different relations with important centres in Europe and elsewhere.

Budapest is the seat of the National Assembly (a single-chamber parliament) and all the important Government offices. Numerous universities, technical schools, museums, libraries and the Hungarian Academy of Science bear witness to the high status of its intellectual life, as do the many theatres and cultural institutions. Budapest is the meeting-place of several parliamentary committees of the Council for Economic Co-operation (RGW/COMECON). In addition, the Hungarian capital is the seat of the Danube Commission and the World Federation of Democratic Youth.

Metropolis

The richest thermal and mineral springs of Europe are to be found in the area of the city of Budapest. Some of them have been used since Celtic times for therapeutic bathing purposes.

Spa

Budapest is in the Central Region of Hungary.

Region

Budapest is situated at 47° 29′ north and 19° 08′ east at a favourable spot for communication across the Danube, leading from Budai hegy-ség (the hills of Buda) on the threshold of the Hungarian Central Uplands, to the north-western edge of the Great Hungarian Plain (Alföld). The highest point of the city area is János-hegy (John's Hill); 529 m (1736 feet), situated in the hills of Buda to the west of the Danube. The lowest point of the city is in the region of Csepel-sziget (the island of Csepel) in the Danube at a height of 97 m (318 feet) above normal water-level.

Geographical Position

Topographical contrasts are a feature of the unique landscape. The territory of the city on the right of the Danube includes the river terraces of various heights and extends far into the Buda upland, which is composed of dolomite and chalk and which was articulated by a tectonic disturbance into a higher northern part (János-hegy, 529 m (1736 feet)) and a lower southern part (Gellért-hegy, 235 m (771 feet)). The plain of Pest on the left bank of the Danube is far more favourable to settlement, and has long been the focus of population of the Hungarian

◄ *Council Building in Pest*

capital. A special place is reserved for the three islands in the river: Obuda-sziget, Margit-sziget and Csepel-sziget.

Telephone Dialling Codes

From Great Britain: 010 361
From the USA and Canada: 011 361

Area

The city covers an area of 525 sq. km (203 sq. miles). About 173 sq. km (67 sq. miles) of the area of the city is on the right bank of the Danube and about 352 sq. km (106 sq. miles) on the left bank. Almost half of the city territory is built up; the remainder consists of open spaces (especially woods, areas of agricultural use and parks). The Hungarians are proud to call their capital the "greenest in Europe". The road network comprises 3700 km (2300 miles). Budapest extends from north to south approximately 25 km (16 miles) and from east to west about 29 km (18 miles).

City Districts

The area of the city is divided into twenty-two districts. On the right bank of the Danube:
Districts I, II, III, XI, XII, XXII
On the left bank of the Danube:
Districts IV, V, VI, VII, VIII, IX, X, XIV, XV, XVI, XVII, XVIII, XIX, XX
Danube Island Csepel:
District XXI
The commercial quarter of the Hungarian capital, which is not dissimilar to the central district of a Western city, is almost entirely within the area of District V (Pest's Danube bank). In little over 2·5 sq. km (1 sq. mile) there are concentrated not only numerous shops, businesses and boutiques which, with their wide range of articles, make Budapest now a leading shopping centre of eastern Europe, but here are also to be found Government administrative offices, financial and trade institutions as well as important cultural and scientific establishments. The density of population of District V is some 19,300 inhabitants per square kilometre (125,000 per sq. mile), with 38,000 workers per square kilometre (98,000 per sq. mile). More than 100,000 employees commute daily into District V. Districts I–III and VI–XIV form the central domiciliary and employment zones. More than 720,000 jobs are located here. The population density amounts to 3240 per square kilometre (1250 per sq. mile). Nearly half a million commuters arrive each day and another 470,000 leave to work elsewhere. The fringe districts IV and XV–XXII comprise the outer domiciliary working districts. As well as modern estates there are large areas of houses with gardens, the majority of which are privately owned. More than half the 230,000 jobs which were set up here were created by modern industrial concerns.

Rebuilding after the Second World War

Towards the end of the Second World War, Budapest suffered heavy destruction. In District I where German troops were holed up for a long time in the castle quarter, almost all the buildings were damaged or destroyed. After the end of the war rebuilding began, but suffered setbacks during the uprising in 1956. From 1960 to 1975 187,000 dwellings were either rebuilt or newly built. In recent years the reconstruction of architectural monuments has been enthusiastically pursued; especially spectacular at present are the plans to rebuild the castle quarter and the reconstruction of buildings in District V.

Buda: view from Fishermen's Bastion over the Castle Palace to Gellért Hill

Population and Religion

Population

In 1720 the three independent towns of Obuda, Buda and Pest had altogether 12,200 inhabitants. At that time the majority of the population lived in Buda. A hundred and ten years later the total population of the three towns had risen to 98,500 and the heaviest concentration had shifted to the Pest side of the river (60,500). When in 1873 the three towns were united to form Budapest, the combined population had already passed the 300,000 mark. After the successful accommodation with Austria in 1867 and the restoration of its position as the capital, Budapest experienced a remarkable upsurge which also resulted in a rapid growth of population. Shortly after the turn of the century a million people lived in Budapest; in the 1970s the 2-million mark was exceeded. On 1 January 1981 the Hungarian capital had 2,064,000 inhabitants, about 20 per cent of the population of the Hungarian People's Republic. Partly owing to changes in the birth rate and the drive to extend the regional lines of communication, the growth of population has recently slowed down considerably, and in addition another contrary development, which has occurred in other cities, has been the movement of people from the inner to the outer districts and to other suburbs of the conurbation. In District V alone, the population has declined between 1960 and today by some 16,000.

Administration

The largely self-governing Hungarian capital is regulated by law. The principal instrument of government is the city council, the members of which are elected every five years. Measures passed by the council are carried out by an executive committee which is led by a president (his position is similar to that of an American state governor). A departmental head governs each specialist department.

Administration of the twenty-two city districts is the responsibility of a district council, the members of which are also elected for five years. The executive committees of the city district are led by chairmen (similar to mayors).

Religion

The majority of the citizens of Budapest who profess a religious belief are traditionally Roman Catholic (at present about 60 per cent). About a quarter are Protestants (the majority of them adherents of the Reformed Church), the others are spread among various religious groups (especially Orthodox and Baptist).

By far the largest number of inhabitants of Budapest are of Magyar descent. Among minorities should be mentioned Gipsies and more especially Germans, Slovakians, Serbs, Croatians and Romanians.

Transport

Local traffic

Every year more than 1·6 million people use the local transport system of Budapest. They are among the most productive of their kind in the world.

The surburban railway (HEV) provides a fast link, with its four routes between the inner city and the smaller centres of Gödöllő, Csepel, Ráckeve and Szentendre on the periphery of the city.

The Underground (Metro) Railway at present has three lines: the first was opened as long ago as 1896, an east–west line came into operation in 1973 and a north-south line in 1979. The Underground system is to be extended.

The Budapest tramway system with its thirty-eight routes forms a very closely meshed network. The trams run at short intervals (on many routes there is a night service).

The most important local means of transport is the bus. In Budapest there are 208 bus and 12 trolley bus routes. A few lines are also in operation at night.

The rack railway up the Széchenyi-hegy, the chair-lift up the János-hegy, the funicular up Castle Hill, the Danube passenger ships and the minibus operating on Margaret Island have more the character of holiday and excursion transport.

Railway

Budapest is an important national and international railway junction. Rail traffic uses four large stations. Throughout the day international trains run between Budapest and all the important European cities. The two principal international express trains are the Orient Express which runs from Berlin via Dresden, Prague, Bratislava, Budapest, Szolnok and Cluj to Bucharest; and the Orient Express from Paris via Strasburg, Stuttgart, Munich and Vienna to Budapest.

Many trains at frequent intervals provide useful connections between Budapest and all the important places in Hungary.

Airport

Budapest's airport, Ferihegy, 14 km (9 miles) south-east of the city centre, is the only international airport in the country. It is served by all the important east and west European airlines. The national Malév airline has services from here to airports in the whole of Europe, North Africa and the Near East. Recently a service was started between Budapest and North America. Because of the rapid development of air traffic in Ferihegy (in 1970 there were 9765 take-offs and landings; in 1979 16,653) the airport is now being modernized and considerably extended. In 1979 Budapest airport handled about 1·8 million passengers. Air freight in the same year accounted for almost 21,000 tonnes (of which air freight leaving Budapest was 15,793 tonnes).

One of the largest ports on the Danube is on the west side of Csepel Island on the southern edge of the city. It has been developed into an international and national free port. In 1979 more than 3 million tonnes of freight was handled; 8 per cent of the entire import for the Hungarian capital was landed in Csepel. The most important goods in 1979 were building materials, fuel, mineral-oil products, ore, food and fodder.

Port

M1: Budapest–Györ (-Bratislava/Vienna)
M3: Budapest–Gyöngyös (–Eger–Miskolc)
M7: Budapest–Lepsény (–Siófok, Balaton)
  2: Budapest–Vác–Parassapuszta (frontier)
  4 (E15): Budapest–Szolnok–Debrecen
  5 (E5): Budapest–Szeged–Röszkö (frontier)
  6: Budapest Erd–Dunaújváros–Paks–Pécs–Barcs (frontier)
10: Budapest–Komárom Györ
11: Budapest–Szentendre–Viségrad–Esztergom
30: Budapest–Gödöllő–Hatvan
70: Budapest–Erd–Székesfehérvár–Lepsény

Motorways and Main Roads

Culture

Budapest is the outstanding cultural centre of Hungary. The seat of the Hungarian Academy of Science, which developed from a successful foundation in 1825 by Count Széchenyi, is here; and most of the colleges and academies of the country are also concentrated in Budapest. Franz Liszt promoted the establishment of the Budapest Academy of Music, which today is world famous. More than two dozen theatres, outstandingly furnished museums and galleries are proof of the reputation of Budapest as a cultural city.

General

Magyar Tudományos Akadémia (Hungary Academy of Science, with ten departments: language and literature, philosophy and history, mathematics and physics, agriculture, medicine, technology, chemistry, biology, law and economics, mining and geology).
Allatorvostudományi Egyetem (Veterinary College).Budapesti Műszaki Egyetem (Technical University of Budapest).
Eötvös Loránd Tudományegyetem (Loránd Eötvös University; a successor to the university founded by Péter Pázmany in Tyrnau in 1635 and moved to Buda in 1777).
Kertészeti Egyetem (Horticultural University).
Marx Károly Közgazdaságtudományi Egyetem (Karl Marx University of National Economy).
Semmelweis Orvostudományi Egyetem (Semmelweis University of Medicine).

Colleges and Academies

Allamigazgatási Fóiskola (College of Administration).

Gyógypedagógiai Tanárképzó Fóiskola (College of Remedial Education).

Kereskedelmi és Vendéglátóipari Fóiskola (College of Trade and Catering).

Külkereskedelmi Fóiskola (College of External Trade).

Liszt Ferenc Zeneművészeti Fóiskola (Franz Liszt Music Academy).

Magyar Iparművészeti Fóiskola (College of Hungarian Arts and Crafts).

Magyar Képzőművészeti Fóiskola (Hungarian College of Fine Art).

Magyar Testnevelési Fóiskola (Hungarian College of Physical Education).

Orvostovábbképző Intézet (Further Education Institute of Medicine).

Pénzügyi és Számviteli Fóiskola (College of Finance).

Szinház és Filmművészeti Fóiskola (College of Drama and Cinematic Art).

Museums and Galleries

Budapest has four museums of international importance. The National Museum (archaeological and historical collection) provides a glimpse into the history of the country. In the Hungarian National Gallery, the Museum of Fine Arts and the Arts and Crafts Museum, masterpieces of Hungarian and European artists can be found. In addition the tourist will find informative exhibitions in the Museums of Ethnography, of Trade and Catering, Agriculture, Military History, the Workers' Movement, Natural Science and Literature, as well as in the Budapest Historical Museum and in over twenty other special collections.

Music and Theatre

Since the last century music has had an important place in Budapest, not least through the work of Franz Liszt. The names of the composers Béla Bartók, Zoltán Kodály and Sándor Szokolay, the conductors Janos Ferencsik, György Lehel and Jenö Ormandy, as well as the pianist György Cziffra (some of the artists named are today living abroad) are evidence of the standard of music in the cultural life of Budapest. The annual major events, the Budapest Spring Festival and Budapest Festival Weeks in the autumn, include important musical contributions. The Redoubt in Pest, the Erkel Theatre and auditoria of the Academy of Music, the Matthias Church, the Synagogue in Dohány Street, the Operetta Theatre and the new sports hall are the venues for a broad and diverse programme. The Hungarian National Philharmonia, the Budapest Philharmonia, the Orhestra of Hungarian Radio and Television, the Budapest Madrigal Ensemble, the Franz Liszt Chamber Orchestra and the Budapest Chamber Ensemble, together with the Schola Hungarica are well known in musical circles outside Hungary.

With more than two dozen theatres, Budapest is among the leading theatrical cities of eastern Europe. Abroad, this reputation is especially represented by the Hungarian State Popular Art Ensemble, which is devoted to the maintenance of cultural assets. The leading theatres are the National Theatre, the Erkel Theatre, the Madách Theatre, the Pest Theatre, the Pest Redoubt, the Castle Theatre, the Josephtown Theatre, the People's Theatre, the Attila-József Theatre, the University

Morning light on the Danube (Parliament Building)

Theatre and the Theatre of Comedy. Ballet, dance and pantomime have a home in the new sports hall.

Trade and Industry

Budapest is one of the leading economic centres of the Warsaw Pack countries. It is the headquarters of several international economic organisations of socialist countries (including Agromasch, Intermetall, Intransmasch). Thanks to its opportunities for employment, the Hungarian capital attracts daily more than 250,000 commuters. Today in Budapest about 1·05 million people are employed, most of them in the industrial sector (over 40 per cent) and the service sector (40 per cent). A feature of the economic structure of the capital is the large proportion of high technological and export-oriented branches of industry (engineering and vehicle manufacture, chemistry, metallurgy, electro-technology and electronics, textiles).

General

A very favourable location, and hence communications, coal supplies in the vicinity and the hard work of the population were and are the main forces behind the economic development of Budapest. After the accommodation with Austria in 1867, Budapest was chosen as the capital and became the site of important industrial enterprises. The industrial combine Ganz (locomotives, machinery, wagons, cranes, ships, etc.) was developed from a foundry established in the middle of the previous century. In 1868 Lázlo Láng from Pressburg laid the foundation of an undertaking which is now the most important

Development

15

combine of eastern Europe. The present-day iron and metal works Csepel, the products of which range from steel pipes to sewing-machines, was founded by B. & M. Weiss in 1893.
Between the two world wars, tool-making, telecommunications and textile manufacture gave a new economic impetus to the city. After the Second World War there was further extension of industry. The provision of raw materials from the USSR made possible not only an extension of capacity for existing branches of industry, but also the setting up of works for the oil and chemical industries. For some time now the Ikarus factory has been in a position to supply buses not only to the countries in eastern Europe, but also to Western customers. Since the 1960s, when the top-heavy nature of Hungarian industry was first recognised, more and more factories have been moved outside the conurbation of Budapest.

Trade Fairs

As one of the leading centres of trade fairs in eastern Europe, Budapest plays a major part in national and international exhibitions and congresses. The necessary space requirements are being met, particularly by the extension of the existing exhibition centre HUNGEXPO in District X. A modern congress centre is at present being erected near the South Station.
Among the important extra regional and regular trade fairs, are the international fairs in May and September/October, BNV (Budapesti Nemzetközi Vásár), as well as the tourist exhibition UTAZAS in March.

Banks

Thanks to its strong economy, Budapest is one of the leading finance centres of eastern Europe. Even a number of Western institutions have set up branches in Budapest, among them the National City Bank of Minneapolis, the Banque Nationale de Paris, the Banco di Sicilia, the Central European International Bank and also the Austrian Creditanstalt Bankverein.

Tourism

The historic spa of Budapest has in recent years developed into one of the most important tourist centres in Europe. In 1983, 14,141 beds in thirty-nine hotels were available, where a considerable number of the ten million visitors to Hungary spent at least one night. It has been reliably estimated that in that year 1·5 million visitors from countries in the West (especially from Austria and West Germany) visited the Hungarian capital.

Trade

Budapest's favourable geographical position, in terms of communications, means that it has long been a centre of trade. This is especially true of the city area of Pest, where today all lines of Hungarian economic management converge. In addition, within the sphere of the countries of eastern Europe, Budapest has a leading place as a shopping centre. More than a dozen large stores and numerous other shops and boutiques between the Danube Quay and the Outer Ring offer a wide range of goods. The central markets of the Hungarian capital are no different from those in Western cities.

Notable Personalities

Arpád, tribal prince of the Magyars who belong to the Finno-Ugrian ethnic group, led his people who moved westwards from an area between the Volga and the Kama, over the Carpathians into present-day Hungary, in about 896.

Arpád
Tribal Prince of the Magyars
(c. 880–907)

Béla Bartók, born in Nagyszentmiklós, is with Franz Liszt and Zoltán Kodály among the most famous Hungarian composers. For many years a Professor of Music in Budapest, he made a name for himself as an impulsive champion of the "new music". His rhythms, chords and melodies are evidence of a keen understanding and knowledge of Hungarian popular music. Bartók did not only write piano pieces, he also composed for orchestras and chamber ensembles. Among his best-known works are the opera "Count Bluebeard's Castle" and the ballet "The Wonderful Mandarin".

Béla Bartók
Composer
(25.3.1881–26.9.1945)

This politician, born in Sojtor, led the moderate liberals of the Reform movement in 1848. After 1849 he led the Address Party (so called from the address which this group made to the Austrian Emperor Franz Joseph), on the initiative of which the accommodation with Austria followed in 1867. This led to the establishment of the Austro-Hungarian monarchy.

Ferenc (Francis) von Deák
Politician and Lawyer
(17.10.1803–29.1.1876)

The Baron, a native of Buda was one of the spiritual leaders of the Hungarian Reform movement of the 1840s. He was twice Minister of Culture and Education (1848 in the Batthyány Cabinet and again in 1867 after the Austro-Hungarian accommodation); he campaigned for the extension of Hungarian primary school education and for equal rights for religious denominations.
In his novels Eötvös dealt with the social conditions of his age.

József (Joseph)
Baron of Eötvös
Writer and Politician
(13.9.1813–2.2.1871)

Loránd of Eötvös, the son of Jozsef Baron of Eötvös, is one of the great personalities to come out of Budapest, where he worked as a Professor of Physics and from 1894 to 1895 was Hungarian Minister of Culture. He became world famous through his studies into the theory of gravitation (the Eötvös effect) and the construction of a new kind of rotary balance.

Loránd (Roland) of Eötvös
Physicist
(27.7.1848–8.4.1919)

Ferenc Erkel, who was born in Békésgyula and who died in Budapest, is one of the best-known composers of his fatherland. Not only did he write the melody of the old Hungarian National Anthem, but also the work "Hunyadi László" which found a place in the history of music as the Hungarian national opera.

Ferenc (Francis) Erkel
Composer
(7.11.1810–15.6.1893)

Greatly venerated in Hungary, St Gellért was a Benedictine monk and sometime Abbot of the Monastery of St Giorgio in Venice. King Stephen I brought him into the country of the Magyars in order that he should instruct his son Emmerich. In about 1030 Gellért became the first Bishop of Csanád. He died in Buda as a martyr and was canonized in 1083.

Szent Gellért
(St Gerhard of Csanád)
Bishop and Martyr
(?–24.9.1046)

The composer Károly Goldmark was born in Keszthely on Lake Balaton. As a composer of opera – his chief work is the "Queen of Sheba" – he was able to combine the ideas of Wagner with elements of French grand opera.

Károly (Karl) Goldmark
Composer
(18.5.1830–2.1.1915)

Notable Personalities

Ferenc von Deák   *József von Eötvös*   *Mór Jókai*

Gyula Illyés
Poet
(2.11.1902)

The poet Gyula Illyés, born in Rácegrespuszta, is one of the most important representatives of lyrical and narrative art of his native country. His work is inspired by influences of the French avant-garde. He is also important as a literary historian and the biographer of Petőfi.

Mór (Maurice) Jókai
Writer
(18.2.1825–5.5.1904)

Born in Komárom, he is considered to be the most important representative of the Romantic movement of Hungarian prose. His works comprise about 200 novels, narratives and short stories. Together with Petőfi he was the leader of the Reform-inspired youth movement of the year 1848 in Buda and Pest.

János Kádár
Politician
(26.5.1912)

Born in Kapoly, this Communist politician was Hungarian Minister of the Interior from 1948 to 1950. In October 1956 he became a member of the Revolutionary Government of Nagy. As First Secretary of the newly formed Hungarian Socialist Workers' Party in 1956 he functioned, after the defeat of the popular uprising, as President from 1956 to 1958 and again from 1961 to 1965. Under his jurisdiction, measures of consolidation were introduced and led to a carefully controlled development of the economy which was to ensure a good position for Hungary within the COMECON group.

Imre Kálmán
Composer
(24.10.1882–30.10.1953)

Imre Kálmán was born in Siófok on the southern shore of Lake Balaton. He made a name as a composer of operetta and was celebrated as such not only in Budapest but also in Vienna and Paris. His best-known operettas are "The Gypsy Princess", "Countess Mariza", "The Circus Princess" and "The Duchess of Chicago".

Zoltán Kodály
Composer and Music
Teacher
(16.12.1882–6.3.1967)

Born in 1882 in Kecskemét, Zoltán Kodály is the most important precursor of the Hungarian music movement which is oriented towards traditional popular music. Kodály worked principally in the Hungarian capital and today is one of the most respected Hungarian musicians. His unique collection of Hungarian folk-songs is very famous.

Lajos (Louis) Kossuth
(19.9.1802–20.3.1894)

This lawyer, born in Monik (Komitat Zemplén), was the leading writer from 1840 to 1844 of the "Pesti Hirlap". He was one of the leading figures of the Hungarian liberals of the revolution

Lajos Kossuth

Franz Liszt

Matthias Corvinus

year 1848/49 and instigated the break with the Viennese administration. As Chairman of the Hungarian National Defence Committee he campaigned strongly for the Honvéd. In 1949 he had to resign his position as administrator of the Hungarian kingdom. He died in Turin.

Franz Liszt who was born in Raiding in Hungary, is today honoured as the most important son of the land of the Danube. He made his début as a concert pianist at the age of nine. He furthered his musical education in Vienna and Paris and in 1842 he was made Director of Music at the Court in Weimar. He was enobled in 1859. Between 1861 and 1869 he lived in Rome where he became head of the Hungarian Music Academy (today the Franz Liszt Music Academy), which had been founded at his instigation. As a composer he concentrated chiefly on symphonic writing, Church music and piano concerti. Among his most important works are the "Hungarian Rhapsodies", the "Années de Pélerinage", the "Hungarian Coronation Mass" and the "Gran Festival Mass". Franz Liszt was also revered as a teacher. Among his many pupils were a number of musicians who became well known, including Alexander Borodin and Friedrich Smetana.

Franz (Ferenc) Liszt
Composer and Pianist
(22.10.1811–31.7.1886)

Born in Budapest, this literary historian and philosopher was, in the time of the Hungarian-Soviet Republic, People's Commissar for Education. In 1945 he was made a professor. In the literary field Lukács gave most attention to the novel and realism. Today he is considered one of the leading Communist intellectuals.

Georg Lukács
Literary Historian and
Philosopher
(13.4.1885–4.6.1971)

Born in Klausenburg, the son of the Turkish conqueror Hunyadi, Corvinus was King of Hungary from 1458–1490. In 1469 he was crowned King of Bohemia. During his reign Buda developed into a leading cultural centre of the Renaissance. Italian painters and scholars worked at his Court. Mátyás I not only founded the Bibliotecha Corviniana, one of the greatest libraries in Europe at that time, he also set up a university in Pressburg and had the royal palace in Buda considerably extended. He died in 1490 in Vienna.

Mátyás (Matthias) I.
Corvinus
King of Hungary
(23.2.1443–6.4.1490)

Notable Personalities

Sándor Petőfi   *Ignác Semmelweis*   *Géza Graf Zichy*

Ferenc (Francis) Molnár
Writer
(12.1.1878–1.4.1952)

Ferenc Molnár, born in Budapest, is the author of many widely read novels and short stories – among them an early novel "The Boys of St Paul's Street". His forte, however, was plays and comedies. Some of his pieces have been box-office hits round the world. Among the best known are "Liliom", "The Swan" and "Play in the Castle". There are many anecdotes and stories about Molnár who died in 1952 in New York.

Péter Pázmány
Archbishop
(4.10.1570–19.3.1637)

Péter Pázmány was born in Grosswardein. In his youth he was brought up as a Calvinist but in 1583 he became a Catholic. In 1616 he became Archbishop of Esztergom and led the Hungarian Counter-Reformation. Also known as a man of letters, he founded the University of Tyrnau in 1635 and this was transferred to Buda under the Empress Maria Theresa.

Sándor (Alexander) Petőfi
Poet and Revolutionary
(1.1.1823–31.7.1849)

Some of the poems of this lyricist from Kiskörös became known to a wide section of the public when he was only twenty-one years old. He was an ardent supporter of the Revolutionary movement of 1848/49. Petőfi composed the poem "Rise up Magyars!" which together with his various revolutionary songs was enthusiastically received. As the adjutant of the Polish General Bem he fought for freedom.

Ferenc (Francis) Rákóczi II
Hungarian Prince
(27.3.1676–8.4.1735)

Rákóczi, a nobleman born in Borsi, was in 1703 at the forefront of the fight for freedom of the Hungarians rebelling against the domination of the House of Habsburg. In 1704 he was elected Prince of Siebenburgen and one year later Prince of Hungary. His freedom movement was defeated and so Rákóczi felt obliged to flee to Turkey. He died in Rodosto on the Sea of Marmara.

Ignác (Ignatius) Philipp
Semmelweis
Physician
(1.7.1818–13.8.1865)

A native of Buda, Semmelweis was a doctor and obstetrician who has gone down in medical history as "the saviour of mothers". He acquired this reputation by discovering the cause of and combating puerperal fever.

István (Stephen) I
King of Hungary
(c. 975–15.8.1038)

István, a scion of the Arpads and the Patron Saint of Hungary, was created King of Hungary at Christmas in the year 1000 with a Crown remitted to him by Pope Sylvester II. He organized a feudal State on the French model. He replaced the old tribal constitution by a county administration. The seat of his government was Gran (Esztergom), where he founded an archbishopric in about 1000. István I was made a saint in 1083.

Pál Szabó, who worked for many years in Budapest, is one of the leading representatives of Hungarian literature. In 1960 he became Vice-president of the International PEN Club. Among his best-known works are "People" and "Liberated Country".

Pál (Paul) Szabó
Writer
(20.3.1894–2.11.1970)

Count Széchenyi is one of the forerunners of the Hungarian Reform movement of the last century. He opposed the freedom from taxation enjoyed by the nobility, demanded the repeal of the guilds and became a champion of the peasantry. He was the founder of the Hungarian Academy of Science and a pioneer of the Danube Steamship Company; in 1848 he became the Minister of Transport in Hungary.

István (Stephen), Count
Széchenyi
Politician
(21.9.1792–8.4.1860)

Born in Budapest, the conductor Széll studied in Vienna and with Reger in Leipzig. He worked in Berlin, Glasgow, New York and Cleveland and was also popular in Salzburg as a guest conductor.

Georg Széll
Conductor
(7.6.1897–31.7.1970)

This Professor of Geography in Budapest became the Hungarian Foreign Minister in 1920 and President from 1920 to 1921. In 1939 he was again named President and conducted the second arbitration with Vienna. He committed suicide when he was unable to prevent the entry of his homeland into the Second World War.

Pál (Paul) Teleki
Geographer and Politician
(1.11.1879–3.4.1941)

Mihály Vörösmarty was one of the most important representatives of Hungarian poetry at the time of the Reform. In his work "Zalans Flight", which appeared in 1900 and was written in German, he glorified the acquisition of land by the Magyars. His "Aufruf" (rallying call) was elevated to the status of a national anthem.

Mihály (Michael)
Vörösmarty
Poet
(1.12.1800–19.11.1855)

Born in Sztára the Count was descended from the old Hungarian aristocratic line of Zichy zu Zich and Vásony-Keö. Although he had lost his right arm at the early age of fourteen in a hunting accident, he studied music and by sheer hard work eventually, as one of Franz Liszt's pupils, became a virtuoso pianist with the left hand. In addition he created his own compositions such as operas (including in 1905–12 a trilogy about the Hungarian national hero Rákóczi), choral works, songs and piano music as well as solo pieces and studies for the left hand. Zichy became President of the Hungarian National Conservatoire and Administrator of the Hungarian Opera House in Budapest.

Géza Count Zichy
Composer
(23.7.1849–14.1.1924)

History of Budapest

Old Stone Age	The earliest known traces of settlements on the Buda bank of the Danube.
Middle and New Stone Age	Numerous finds confirm a continuous human activity on the Buda side of the Danube.
2nd c. B.C.	Both banks of the Danube are settled.
Bronze Age	In the entire area of the present-day Hungarian capital several urn sites have been uncovered.
6th c. B.C.	Nomadic Scythian tribes from the area of the Black Sea settle in the area of Budapest.
4th–3rd c. B.C.	Celtic Eraviscs emerge as settlers.
2nd c. A.D.	The Roman fortress of Aquincum, situated in what is now the district of Obuda, becomes the capital of the Province of Pannonia Inferior. Aquincum, which was divided into a military town and a civil town, reached its heyday at the end of the 2nd c.
5th c.	The Huns capture Aquincum. King Attila (Etzel) sets up a great kingdom.
6th–9th c.	The Avars settle by the Danube.
c. 896	The Magyars belonging to the Finno-Ugrian ethnic group led by Prince Arpád press upstream along the Danube from the Carpathians and settle in the area of present-day Obuda.
1000	István (Stephen) I becomes King of Hungary. He organises a feudal State on the Central European model and introduces Christianity. His residences are at Esztergom (Gran) and Székesfehérvár.
12th c.	Merchants from central and west Europe settle in Buda and Pest.
1241–42	Mongols storm the rising Danube cities of Buda and Pest.
1270	Construction of the Castle of Buda ordered by King Béla IV is completed.
1255	Buda receives a market charter.
14th c.	The House of Anjou inherits the Hungarian throne.
1342–82	Lajos (Louis) I (the Great) reigns as king. He has a magnificent palace erected on Castle Hill. Under his leadership the Hungarian sphere of influence extents to Bosnia, Serbia, Bulgaria and into Wallachia.
1387–1437	Sigismund of Luxemburg, later the German Emperor, reigns in Hungary.
1458–90	Mátyás Hunyadi (Matthias Corvinus), son of the Turkish

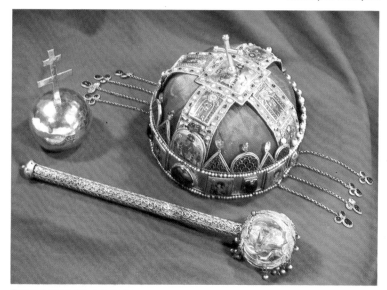

The Hungarian Royal Insignia

conqueror János Hunyadi, is King of Hungary. During his reign Buda develops into a centre of Renaissance culture. The Royal Palace in Buda is extended. With the Bibliotheca Corviniana, one of the greatest libraries of Europe is established.

György Dózsa assembles a peasant army outside Pest with the object of attacking the despotic rule of the nobility.	1514
After their victory over the Hungarian troops at Mohács, the Turks temporarily occupy the Castle of Buda.	1526
Under Sultan Süleyman I (the Magnificent) the Turks control Buda and Pest. At this period many churches are converted into mosques, defensive works renewed and fine bath-houses constructed. Buda is the seat of a Vizier.	1541–1686
Charles of Lorraine retakes Obuda, Buda and Pest for the House of Habsburg.	1686
Resistance against the rule of the Habsburg Emperor of Vienna.	End 17th/beginning 18th c.
Various measures taken by the Empress Maria Theresa lead to a modest economic upsurge. In the meantime a considerable number of German-speaking settlers arrive in Buda and Pest.	1740–80
Bloody defeat of the Hungarian Jacobins.	1795
The University of Tyrnau (Nagyszombat) is moved to Buda. It is the only college of its kind in Hungary. Seven years later it is transferred to Pest.	1797

Old drawing of Buda and Pest in 1617

1825	Foundation of a scientific society as the precursor of the now famous Hungarian Academy of Science.
1837	Building of the National Theatre.
1838	After a disasterous flood of the Danube there follows a comprehensive redevelopment.
1st half 19th c.	Pest becomes a thriving economic centre where trade in grain flourishes in particular.
1848–49	Civil revolution led by liberal nobles and a struggle for freedom against the Austrian hegemony. Count Lajos Batthyány forms a Hungarian government responsible to the State's Parliament. Lajos Kossuth rises to be the most important political leader; the poet Sándor Petöfi, a fervent revolutionary, dies during the struggle for freedom.
1849	The Chain Bridge is opened to traffic.
1867	Accommodation with the ruling Austrian house through the mediation of Ferenc Deák. Emperor Franz Joseph II is crowned King of Hungary in Matthias Church. The Austro-Hungarian monarchy of the Danube comes into being.
1872	Obuda, Buda and Pest are combined into a city.
1887	The first tram runs in Budapest.
1896	Festivities marking the 1000-year existence of Hungary.
1902	The Parliament Building is completed.

A considerable number of industrial undertakings are established in Budapest. The contours of a "Ruhr district by the Danube" are drawn up.	Beginning of the 20th c.
Economic and social defects lead to unrest which culminates in strikes and demonstrations; on 23 May, "blood-red Thursday", these are ended by force.	1912
First World War. Budapest suffers severe setbacks in its economic development.	1914–18
The Republic is proclaimed.	16.11.1918
A Soviet Republic, established in March and supported by Social Democrats and Communists is only able to last for a few months. In November Miklós Horthy seizes power.	1919
First transmission of Budapest Radio.	1925
Large workers' demonstrations.	1930
Hungary enters the Second World War on the side of Germany.	1941
The turmoil of war influences life in the Hungarian capital. Horthy is locked up by the National Socialists. In autumn Budapest becomes a front-line town and suffers severe damage, especially in the castle quarter where units of the German army are barricaded in.	1944
From now on Soviet units control the whole of Budapest.	13.2.1945

View from Castle Hill over the Danube

History of Budapest

1946	The Freedom Bridge is opened to traffic.
20.8.1949	The new Hungarian constitution comes into force. 20 August becomes a national holiday.
1950	By a administrative reform the area of Budapest is considerably extended. Opening of the Ferihegy Airport.
1953	Completion of the Nép Stadium.
1956	Political and economic abuses fuel a popular uprising in autumn. This leads to heavy fighting between the rebels and the Government troops and with Soviet units. The inner city presents a picture of devastation. János Kádár, First Secretary of the newly founded Workers' Party, introduces measures of consolidation and gives an impulse for a carefully increased development of the economy.
1958	Inauguration of the television transmitter on the Széchenyi-hegy.
1964	The Elisabeth Bridge is opened to traffic.
1960–80	Development of a comprehensive programme of civic building and extension of the local transport system (especially the Underground network).
1975–84	Exemplary renovation of protected buildings. Opening of several large luxury hotels.
1983	Budapest is the venue for the world gymnastic championships.
1984	Conference of the Foreign Ministers of members of the Warsaw Pact. The sixth full assembly of the World Lutheran Federation.

Parliament Building overlooking the Danube

26

Budapest from A to Z

Academy of Music

See Franz Liszt Academy of Music

Academy of Science

See Roosevelt tér

Academy Utca

See Roosevelt tér

Agricultural Museum

See City Woodland Park

Alagút

See Chain Bridge

Alfréd Hajós Baths

See Margaret Island

Allami Opera House

See State Opera

Angyalföld   D–H 1–3

Underground Station
M3 (Elmunkás tér)

Trams
3V, 12, 14, 33V, 55, 75, 76,
79

Buses
4, 15, 20, 26, 30, 32, 33, 43,
43A, 55, 84, 120

The district of Angyalföld, lying in the north of Pest was, until
the Second World War, a sombre industrial suburb. Since the
1950s a modern district has arisen here.
By the busy Elmunkás tér stands the Church of St Margaret
built in 1922 by István Möller. Behind lies a large market.
Farther to the north the Attila József Theatre (1950; Váci út 63)
can be found.
A monument commemorating the poet József Attila (1955 by
A. Beck) stands on József Attila Square.

The Island of Nép-sziget in the Danube off Angyaföld is principally used for relaxation and recreation. Rowing regattas often take place in the blocked-off arm of the Danube.

Nép-sziget Danube Island

See Practical Information, Spas.

Szabadság-fürdő

Anjou Bastion

See Buda, Important Streets and Squares, Bécsi kapu tér

Anonymous Monument

See City Woodland Park

Aquincum

See Obuda

Archduke Joseph Square

See József Nádor tér

Arpád Bridge (Arpád-hid)   D1

Almost 1 km in length and the most northerly of the Budapest road bridges, Arpád Bridge which crosses the northern tip of Margaret Island (see entry), links the districts of Buda and Angyalföld (see entries). Its construction was begun in 1939 and it was opened to traffic in 1950.
Additional construction work since 1983 has made the bridge an important link in the road system of Budapest.

Location
Obuda-Angyalföld

Tram
33V

Buses
55, 84

Art Gallery

See Heroes' Square

Artists' Promenade

See Margaret Island

Bajcsy-Zsilinszky út

See Inner Ring

◀ *Matthias Church in Buda*

Basilica

See St Stephen's Basilica

Batthyány Palace

See Outer Ring, Lenin körút

Batthyány tér

See Viziváros

Bécsi kapu tér

See Buda, Important Streets and Squares

Béla-Komjádi Swimming Pool

See Imperial Baths and Luke's Baths

Béla-Lajta House

See Martinelli tér

Bem József tér

See Viziváros

Biermann István tér

See Martinelli tér

Blaha Lujza tér

See Outer Ring

Botanical Garden of the University (Füvészkert) G6

Location
Korányi Sándor u.

Laid out in 1847, and originally quite extensive, the Botanical Garden of the University became more and more restricted in size by the continuing extension of built-up areas in the

A particularly charming Baroque church stands in the old village square; it was completed in 1756. Features of the interior are an altar-painting by Altomonte and a pulpit in Rococo style. Also of note are sculptures dating from the time when the church was built.

Baroque church

Near the church, Péter-Pál utca goes uphill and along it a number of buildings from former centuries have been preserved.

In the cemetery of Budafok, south-west of the church, there are beautiful Baroque and Classical tombstones.

The headquarters of the National Wine Producers (Allami pincegazdaságok; Kossuth Lajos utca 84) and the Budafok Wine Producers (Budafoki Pincegazdaság) still make use of part of the considerable network of cellars and tunnels. A wine cellar furnished in the traditional manner is the Borkatakomba (Nagytétényi út 63).

Wine Cellars (viewing by appointment)

Many of the cellars were at one time lived in. This is very clearly demonstrated in the cellar in Veréb u. 4.

Budapest Historical Museum

See Castle Palace

---

*Buda Upland (Budai-hegység)   A1–8(K/L1/2)

The Buda Upland forms the natural western boundary of the Hungarian capital. The hills, consisting of dolomite, chalk, clay and marl are, for the most part, wooded and have long been popular as a local recreation area with the inhabitants of Budapest. A close network of paths, fine scenery, facilities for games and sports, a pioneer railway, cafés, etc., testify to the attractions of this beautiful upland area.
Buses: D, H, J, 28, 29, 65, 158.

Location
To the west of the town

Cog-wheel Railway
Város major–Széchenyi-hegy

Chair-lift
Zugliget–János-hegy

The Three Frontier Hill (497 m (1631 ft)) rises to the north within the boundary of Budapest. From its almost bare summit there is a fine view of Obuda. Below the top of the hill to the north-east can be seen the strange Guckler rock (Guckler-szikla). Two kilometres (1 mile) north-north-west (as the crow flies) from the Three Frontier Hill rises Csúcs-hegy (445 m (1460 ft); good view). Below to the south in Paul's Valley is a stalactitic cave (Pálvögyi cseppkőbarlang) which is well worth visiting.

Three Frontier Hill
(Hármashatár-hegy)

János-hegy rises in the west of Buda. It is the highest eminence in the Hungarian capital (529 m (1736 ft)). From the almost 24 m (79 ft) high observation tower there is a magnificent view. János-hegy has also been made attractive for winter-sports enthusiasts by the installation of a chair-lift, a ski-jump, a piste and a ski-lift.

János-hegy
(John's Hill)

From Városmajor Park (see entry) a cog-wheel railway, which was planned in the 19th c., ascends Szabadság-hegy and Széchenyi-hegy (439 m (1441 ft); transmitter of Hungarian

Szabadság-hegy
(Freedom Hill) and
Széchenyi-hegy

Television). Up here are several nursing-homes and tourist hotels. A narrow-gauge pioneer railway opened in 1951 and staffed by children and young people under the supervision of adults, provides an excursion into this especially charming scenic part of the Buda Upland.

Café Gerbeaud

See Vörösmarty tér

Café Hungária

See Outer Ring, Lenin körút

Café Ruszwurm

See Buda, Important Streets and Squares, Szentháromság utca

Calvin Square

See Inner Ring, Kálvin tér

Castle

See Buda
See Castle Palace

Castle Museum

See Castle Palace

Castle Museum Nagytétény

See Nagytétény

Castle Palace (Várpalota)   C5(M/N8)

Location
South spur of Castle Hill

Buses
V, 16, 16A

Funicular Railway
Clark Adám tér–Vár

The magnificent Castle Palace of Buda, the origins of which go back to the 13th c., occupies the southern spur of Castle Hill. The extensive buildings, from which there are excellent views, are the former residence of the Hungarian kings, but they were severely damaged in the Second World War, and lengthy rebuilding was necessary. A great part of the palace buildings today appear in new splendour and provide room for important museums and other cultural facilities.

Buda

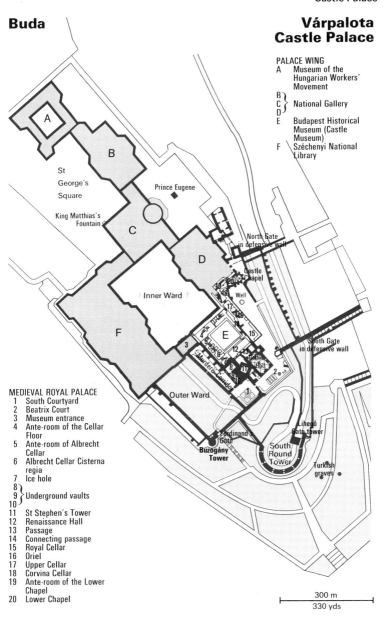

PALACE WING
A   Museum of the Hungarian Workers' Movement
B ⎫
C ⎬ National Gallery
D ⎭
E   Budapest Historical Museum (Castle Museum)
F   Széchenyi National Library

St George's Square

Prince Eugene

King Matthias's Fountain

North Gate in defensive wall

Castle Chapel

Inner Ward

Well

South Gate in defensive wall

F

E

3

Murderer's Corridor

Gothic Hall

Outer Ward

Ferdinand's Gate

Buzogány Tower

South Round Tower

Lihegő Gate tower

Turkish graves

MEDIEVAL ROYAL PALACE
1   South Courtyard
2   Beatrix Court
3   Museum entrance
4   Ante-room of the Cellar Floor
5   Ante-room of Albrecht Cellar
6   Albrecht Cellar Cisterna regia
7   Ice hole
8 ⎫
9 ⎬ Underground vaults
10 ⎭
11 St Stephen's Tower
12 Renaissance Hall
13 Passage
14 Connecting passage
15 Royal Cellar
16 Oriel
17 Upper Cellar
18 Corvina Cellar
19 Ante-room of the Lower Chapel
20 Lower Chapel

300 m

330 yds

Castle Palace

History of the building

The first castle was built by King Béla IV in the 13th c. Its purpose was to provide protection from attacks by Tartars and Mongols. Unfortunately nothing remains of this building.

Under King Karl Robert a smaller palace was erected in the 14th c. King Sigismund, who made Buda his residence, had a Gothic castle built, which was considerably extended, in Renaissance style, under Matthias Corvinus.

Although the Castle Palace remained during the time of Turkish occupation, it was nevertheless ruined during the Siege of 1686. Therefore, in the 18th c. a new castle was built, which in the time of the Empress Maria Theresa had more than 200 rooms. The Castle Palace, from now on the residence of the Palatine (the representative of the Habsburg overlords), was rebuilt by the architects Hauszmann and Ybl in Neo-Baroque style. A symmetrical layout was created which is oriented to the central dome facing the Danube.

Museum of the Hungarian Workers' Movement
(Magyar Munkásmozgalmi Múzeum; Wing A)

Since 1977 the Museum of the Hungarian Workers' Movement has been housed in the northern wing A. It contains interesting documents, materials and objects from workshops as well as furnishings from workers' dwellings which illustrate the life and the culture of the Hungarian workers since the middle of the 19th c.

Szent György tér (St George's Square)

In St George's Square stands a beautiful ornamental fountain designed by A. Stróbl; it shows King Matthias hunting.

*Hungarian National Gallery (Magyar Nemzeti Galéria; Wings B, C, D)

The Hungarian National Gallery occupies the three main wings of the castle and is still in the process of being built up. At the present time the following exhibits are to be seen:

Romantic and Gothic

Sculpture; frescoes; reproductions from the age of the foundation of the State; triptychs; sculptures and panels, including the "Madonna Szlatvini", the "Madonna of Toporci" and the Altars of Jánosréti.

Renaissance

Sculpture, including the "Madonna of Diósgyori" and works of art from the Parish Church of the Inner City of Pest.

Late Renaissance and Baroque

Carving by Jakob Bogdány, Adám Mányoki as well as by Maulbertsch and his contemporaries; works of art of the Hungarian Age of Enlightenment; Late Baroque paintings and Baroque monumental sculpture.

19th c. paintings

Works by Károly Markó, Miklós Barabás, József Borsos, Géza Mészöly, Károly Lotz, Bertalan Székely, Merse Pál Szinyei, etc; paintings by Bálint Kiss, Viktor Madarász, Mór Than, Gyula Benczur, etc; separately but in chronological order: paintings by Mihály Munkácsy (including "Christ Before Pilate", "A Woman Collecting Faggots") and László Paál (especially landscapes).

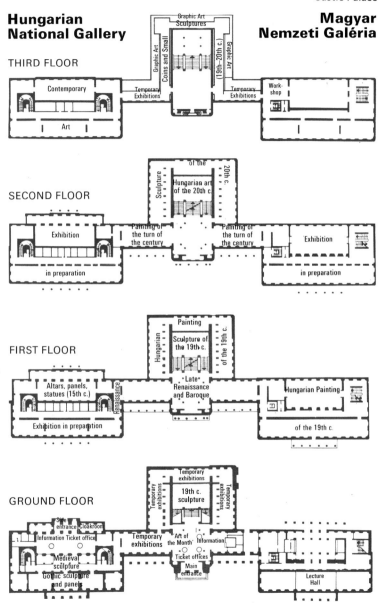

Castle Palace

Hungarian
National Gallery

Magyar
Nemzeti Galéria

THIRD FLOOR

Graphic Art
Sculptures

Graphic Art

Coins and Small

(19th–20th c.)

Graphic Art

Contemporary

Temporary
Exhibitions

Temporary
Exhibitions

Work-
shop

Art

SECOND FLOOR

Sculpture

of the

Hungarian art
of the 20th c.

20th c.

Exhibition

Painting of
the turn of
the century

Painting of
the turn of
the century

Exhibition

in preparation

in preparation

FIRST FLOOR

Painting

Hungarian

Sculpture of
the 19th c.

of the 19th c.

Altars, panels,
statues (15th c.)

Renaissance

Late
Renaissance
and Baroque

Hungarian Painting

Exhibition in preparation

of the 19th c.

GROUND FLOOR

Temporary
exhibitions

Temporary
exhibitions

19th c.
sculpture

Temporary
exhibitions

Side
entrance Cloakroom

Information Ticket office

Temporary
exhibitions

Art of
the Month

Information

Medieval
sculpture

Ticket offices

Gothic sculpture
and panels

Main
entrance

Lecture
Hall

39

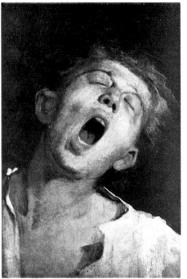

Mihály Munkácsy "Laughing pupil" (1868) and "Woman churning butter" (1873)

Béla Uitz "Woman in white" (1918)

Sándor Bortnyk: "Red fabric" (1919)

Works of art by Miklós Izsó, Alajos Stróbl, György Zala, János Fadrusz as well as some less-well-known masters.	19th c. sculpture
Paintings by Simon Hollosy, János Thoma, József Réti as well as works by members of the Nagybányai artists' colony (among them Károly Ferenczy).	Painting of the turn of the century
under reorganisation.	20th c. painting
Works by Ferenc Medgyessy, László Mészáros, Pál Pátzay, Miklós Borsos and Ö. F. Beck.	20th c. sculpture
under reorganisation.	Coins, etc
under reorganisation.	Graphical collection

Equestrian Statue of Prince Eugene

In front of the domed building, on the side facing the Danube, is a bronze equestrian statue by József Róna (1900), representing Prince Eugene of Savoy who opposed the Turks.

Széchenyi National Library (Wing F)

The Széchenyi National Library is at present being moved from the Hungarian National Museum (see entry) to Wing F of the Castle Palace. This institution, founded by Count Ferenc Széchenyi in 1802, contains about 2 million books and more than 350,000 manuscripts.

*Budapest Historical Museum
(Budapesti Történeti Múzeum; City Museum, Castle Museum; E Wing)

Wing E of the Castle Palace houses the Budapest Historical Museum. It contains highly interesting documents, wrought-iron work, ceramics, textiles, household utensils and other objects which provide a comprehensive picture of the life and development of the Hungarian capital in the independent towns of Obuda, Buda and Pest up to 1872.
In the ante-room of the basement is a model of the medieval Royal Palace. In the adjoining rooms of the medieval castle, partly reconstructed, can be seen sculpture and carving, stove tiles, kitchen utensils and weapons from the Royal Palace of the 14th and 15th c.
In the Renaissance Room is a picture showing Matthias Corvinus and Beatrice of Aragon, his second wife. The floor-tiles (majolica) are extremely beautiful. In the Gothic Room are fine sculptures of the 14th c. Valuable 14th c. figures of saints can be seen in the Chapel of the Castle Palace as well as a 15th c. triptych. In the lower cellar are architectural elements also of the 15th c.

Prince Eugene

Remains of the Medieval Castle

Below Wings E and F of the Castle Palace lie parts of the medieval castle complex, at present under reconstruction. The

Buzogány Tower (buzogány = morning star or club) is impressive as is the Ferdinand Gate. Outside is the South Tower which was in existence in the 15th and 16th c.
Outside the walls of the castle a number of Turkish tombstones can still be seen.

Castle Theatre

See Buda, Important Streets and Squares, Disz tér

Castle Vajdahunyad

See City Woodland Park

Castle Zichy

See Obuda

Cella trichora

See Obuda

Central Market Hall

See Dimitrov tér

Chain Bridge (Széchenyi-lánchid)   C5(N7)

The Chain Bridge, one of the landmarks of the Hungarian capital, was constructed between 1838 and 1849 by the English engineers William Tierny Clark and Adam Clark. The bridge, 375 m (410 yd) long and almost 16 m (18 yd) wide is supported by chains fixed to 48 m (158 ft) high towers at either end. At the ends of the bridge stand stone lions by J. Marschalkó. The bridge was destroyed in the Second World War, but in 1949 was again opened to traffic.
At the Buda end of the bridge lies Clark Adám tér, which in 1971 received the 0–km–stone by Miklós Borsos, the symbol from which distances along main roads from Budapest are measured. Close by is the funicular, dating from 1870, but at present being renovated, up to the Castle District.

Buses
2, 4, 16

From the Buda end of the Chain Bridge the Alagút, a road tunnel about 350 m (380 yd) long and which was constructed in 1857, leads to Krisztinaváros (Christian Town).

Alagút

◄ *Winged altar in the Castle chapel*

Chain Bridge and Castle Palace after dark

China Museum (Kina Múzeum) F4

Location
Gorkij fasor 12

Trolleybus
78

Bus
33

The China Museum, which developed from the China collection of the Ferenc-Hopp Museum of East-Asian Art (see entry), provides a good survey of Chinese art. Among the most beautiful exhibits, some of which are several hundred years old, are works of bronze, ivory and china. The textile collection is also of great interest.
Numerous visitors are attracted by the temporary exhibitions on various themes which are mounted throughout the year.
Opening times: Tues.–Sun. 10 a.m.–6 p.m.

Reformed Church
(Reformation templom)

Close at hand (Gorkij fasor 5–7) is the Reformed Church (1913; architect A. Arkay) in Secessionist style; the principal façade is decorated with beautiful majolica work.

Circus

See City Woodland Park, Municipal Circus

Citadel

See Gellért Hill

Vajdahunyad Castle in the City Woodland Park

City Museum

See Castle Palace, Budapest Historical Museum

*City Woodland Park (Városliget)   F/G3/4

The Városliget (City Woodland Park) with its pretty lake, is the second largest of its kind in the Hungarian capital. Extending over more than 1 sq. km (0·38 sq. mile), the area was laid out in the 19th c. according to the ideas of the French landscape-gardener Nebbion. The Városliget has become a major attraction for the public through its cultural and recreational facilities – Zoological-Botanical Garden, pleasure park, Museum of Fine Art, art gallery, Civic Circus, Széchenyi Baths, Vajdahunyad Castle with the Agricultural Museum, Transport Museum, Arena Theatre, sports hall, games and sports grounds, garden for the blind.

Location
District XIV

Underground Station
M1 (Hősök tere, Széchenyi fürdő)

Trolleybuses
70, 72, 74, 75, 79

Buses
1, 4, 4A, 20, 30, 55, 120

*Castle Vajdahunyad (Vajdahunyad vára)   F3

The castle was built in 1896 by I. Alpár (monument outside the entrance) on the occasion of the millennium festival. In his work the architect tried to combine several architectural features which are characteristic of Hungary. The greater part of the building complex was designed on the model of the castle of the Turkish conqueror Hunyadi, which can be seen in the present-day Romanian town of Hunedoara.

Location
On the island in the lake

Opening times
Tues.–Sun. 10 a.m.–6 p.m.

45

"Anonymous" Memorial

Alpár Monument

The castle entrance has affinities with Gothic architecture; on the left it is flanked by a copy of a tower in Upper Hungary, on the right by a tower which is reminiscent of its model in Sighisoara in Romania. At the back of the Romanesque wing on the east side of the castle courtyard is a chapel, which was designed on the model of the Benedictine church in Jak in western Hungary. Stylistic elements from north Hungary and Siebenburgen characterise the appearance of the part of the building on the right at the back of the castle entrance. A Renaissance wing forms a link with the palace in Baroque style which contains the Agricultural Museum.

Agricultural Museum

The Agricultural Museum (Mezőgazdasági Múzeum), housed in the Baroque Palace of Castle Vajdahunyad, provides a very good survey of the various facets of Hungarian agriculture. On show are implements of rural handcraft and machines for lightening the load of farming, documents about the raising of animals (especially horses, cattle, sheep and pigs), the production and storage of wine, forestry, as well as hunting (there is a fine collection of trophies) and fishing. Periodic special exhibitions complement the museum programme.

Anonymous Monument

In the south-eastern courtyard of Castle Vajdahunyad stands a memorial, created in 1903 by Miklós Ligeti, honouring Anonymous, an unknown historical scribe of the 12th/13th c., who, it is believed, composed the first Hungarian chronicle.

Zoological-Botanical Garden (Fővárosi Allat-és Növénykert)   F3

Location
XIV, Allatkerti Körút 6–12

The Budapest Zoological-Botanical Garden is situated in the north-west part of Városliget. It was laid out in the 1860s and has since been very popular with the citizens of Budapest. Some of the indigenous and exotic animals (approximately 500 species) occupy enclosures in the open which were designed to resemble their natural habitat, as are the terrariums, aquariums and other purpose-made buildings. Among the attractions are the birds of prey cage, the rock garden, the polar bear and sealion pool, the children's zoo, the monkey house, the caves for lions and bears, the Africa house and the pachyderm house.

Interested visitors can study the flora of temperate latitudes along the paths; tropical plants can be found in the palm house as well as in the terrariums and aquariums for animals from hot countries.

Trolleybus
72

Civic Circus (Fóvárosi Nagycirkusz)   F3

The new building of the Civic Circus, opened in 1971, is situated on the eastern edge of the zoo area, opposite the Széchenyi Baths; it is one of the most popular institutions of its kind in Europe. All the well-known circuses of the world have performed and still perform here. The circus tradition in Városliget goes back to 1891 when the first performances were staged.

Location
XIV, Allatkerti körút 7

Trolleybus
72

Pleasure Park (Vidám Park)   F/G3

Every year many thousands of visitors come to the Budapest Tivoli. This is a pleasure park with a giant wheel, a big dipper and various rides as well as numerous other diversions.

Location
XIV, Allatkerti körút 14–16

Trolleybus: 72

*Széchenyi Baths (Széchenyi-fürdő)   F3

The complex of the Széchenyi Baths in the northern part of Városliget comprises an open-air bath and a covered bath in Neo-Baroque style with steam and normal baths. The warm water (over 70 °C (158 °F) comes from a spring discovered in the previous century.

Location
XIV, Allatkerti körút 11

Underground Station
M1 (Széchenyi-fürdő)

Transport Museum (Közlekedési Múzeum)   G3

In a building constructed for the purpose in Városliget are the exhibits of the Hungarian Transport Museum. The development of transport from ancient times until today is very clearly portrayed. Models of old Danube and Lake Balaton vessels are included in the exhibition as are various locomotives and aircraft (record-breaking aircraft and helicopters). Outside the museum can be seen an old dining-car. In front of the museum is a children's area.

Location
Május 1 út 26

Trolleybus
72, 74

Congress Centre   B6

Two kilometres (1·25 miles) south-west of the town, close to the Hotel Novotel Budapest, a modern congress centre is under

Location
Hegyalja út

Tram
61

Buses
8, 8A, 12, 112

construction. The conference facilities (the actual space for meetings covers 3000 sq. m (32,300 sq. ft) comprises a large hall seating 2,000, a medium-size hall for 200 and six other rooms which can hold up to 40 people each. The technological conference equipment is, of course, designed according to the most modern ideas.

Information

Budapest Congress Centrum, tel: 6 67 56.

Contra Aquincum

See Március 15 tér

Corvin tér

See Viziváros

Csepel (Csepel-sziget)

HÉV stop
2 (Csepel)

Buses
38, 38A, 38B, 48, 51, 52, 52A, 59, 59A, 71, 148, 159

Csepel, District XXI of the Hungarian capital, is situated on an island on the Danube and is the headquarters of the Csepel Vas-és Fémművek (Csepel Iron and Metal Works), with many thousand employees. This undertaking, established by B. & M. Weiss in 1893 produces goods ranging from steel pipes to bicycles.

Szabadkikötö
(Free Port)

A modern Free Port lying on the west side of Csepel Island. In 1979 the turnover of goods in this huge Free Port on the Danube was more than 3 million tonnes.

Csepel strandfürdő
(Swimming-bath)

The riverside swimming-bath of Csepel, fed by a thermal spring, is the third largest of its kind in Budapest. It is situated on the Soroksári Duna, a branch of the river on the east side of Csepel Island. Opposite lies the little island of Molnár-sziget.

*Danube

Boat Trips
from landing stages at Vigadó tér and Bem József tér

The Danube (Hungarian Duna) flows through Budapest from north to south; within the city boundaries its widest place 640 m (700 yds) is in the north of the city just below the junction of the two arms of the river which enclose the island of Szentendre (Szentendrei-sziget). The river is at its narrowest 283 m (310 yds) below Gellért Hill; here it is about 9 m (30 ft) deep.

Flooding

Until the late 19th century rises in the water level led to considerable insecurity in the districts near the Danube. Then the width of the river could exceed 1000 m (1100 yds), and in the lower lying parts of the city considerable damage could be caused. Therefore in the second half of the last century measures to regulate the flow of the water were urgently put in hand.

Industry on the Danube

Central Market Hall in Dimitrov tér

With the expansion of industry in Budapest and in locations further upstream, the Danube became of increasing importance for the movement of goods, and in the preceeding century the capacity of the port installations of the island of Csepel (Csepel-sziget) – see entry – was considerably increased. Along the Danube Corso on the Pest bank landing stages for national and international passenger ships were built and these were heavily used.

Waterway

The Danube is at present spanned by two railway bridges (the New Pest Bridge and the South Rail Bridge) and by six road bridges (Margaret Bridge, Petőfi Bridge, and – see entries – Arpad Bridge, Chain Bridge, Elisabeth Bridge and Freedom Bridge).

Bridges

*Danube Bend (or Danube Knee; Dunakanyar)

The Danube Bend between Esztergom and Szentendre (see entries) is one of the most delightful scenic reaches of the whole course of the river and is often referred to as the "Hungarian Wachau". Wildly romantic landscapes, remains of Roman and medieval fortifications, venerable little towns and magnificent views attract thousands of tourists every year.
Here the Danube breaks through the threshold of the Hungarian Central Uplands. On the right bank rise the foothills of the Bakony Forest, notably the Pilis range (Pilis-hegység) which reaches a height of 757 m (2480 ft). From the north the Börzsöny Mountains (Börzsöny-hegység), up to 865 m

Location
20–60 km (12–17 miles) north and north-west of Budapest

Route
Main road No. 11 Budapest–Szentendre–Visegrád–Esztergom
Main road No. 2 Budapest–Vác

49

Danube Corso

Buses
From Engels tér, Budapest

Suburban Railway HEV
Budapest-Szentendre
(from Batthyány tér,
Budapest)

Boat trips
From Vigado tér, Budapest

(2839 ft), slope down towards the river. The Danube now follows a channel defined by structural movement in bends and a definite loop near Visegrád (see entry); shortly before reaching Vác (see entry) it divides into two arms (Island of Szentendre) and from its previous west–east direction it now turns to the south (the river's "knee").

Today the "Hungarian Wachau" and the hills which border it are the favourite recreational area of Hungary after Lake Balaton. It is provided with areas of holiday homes, camp sites, numerous inns and hotels.
See Esztergom
See Szentendre
See Vác
See Visegrád

Danube Corso (Dunakorzó)   D5(L4/5)

Trams
2, 2A

Buses
2, 15

The bank of the Danube on the Pest side of the river between the Chain Bridge and Elisabeth Bridge is locally known as the "Danube Corso" (Dunakorzó). From here, especially in the evening when the lights are on, there is a fantastic view of the Fishermen's Bastion, the Matthias Church, the Castle Palace, the Gellért Monument, the Citadel and the Freedom Monument on Gellért Hill.

Deák Ferenc tér

See Inner Ring

Dimitrov tér   D/E6(M5/6)

Trams: 2, 2A, 47, 49

Trolleybus: 83

Buses: 1, 15, 109

The square at the Pest end of Freedom Bridge is named after Georgii Dimitroff, a Bulgarian pioneer of the Workers' Movement. In the square is a monument to Dimitroff by J. Kraschmaroff (1954), as well as a memorial to the fallen.

Central Market Hall

On the south side of the square stands the Central Market Hall (Központi vásárcsarnok), built by Sam. Petz in Neo-Gothic style. Near by is the Foodstuffs Exchange (completed in 1896) which has survived until the present, as the numerous foods (fruit and vegetables, spices, meat and sausage, pastry, fish, etc.) testify. Even arts and crafts, textiles (hand-embroidered blouses and basketwork) can be obtained here.

Karl Marx University

A short distance to the south can be found the Karl Marx University of Economic Science (Marx Károly Közgazdaság-tudományi Egyetem). It is housed in the former Central Customs Office, built between 1870–1874 by Ybl in Neo-Renaissance style. The magnificent former Gala Court of the building, which is 170 m (558 ft) long, was converted into an assembly hall.

East Station

Disz tér

See Buda, Important Streets and Squares

Dominican Convent

See Margaret Island

Duna

See Danube

East Station (Keleti pályaudvar)   G5

The East Station is the largest and most important of the Budapest stations. Most of the international express trains which traverse Hungarian territory stop here.
The architecture of this main station is very fine; it was completed in 1884 to the plans of J. Feketeházy and G. Rochlitz and has been renovated several times since. The main façade in Neo-Renaissance style is adorned with two statues representing James Watt and George Stephenson.

Location
VIII, Baross tér

Underground Station
M2 (Baross tér)

Trams
23, 24, 36, 44, 67

Elisabeth Bridge

Elisabeth Bridge

Trolleybus
73, 76, 80

Buses
7, 7A, 33, 78, 95

Murals by K. Lotz and M. Than embellish the prestigious station hall.
In the square outside the station stands a Gábor-Baross Memorial (A. Szécsi; 1898) in honour of the former Trade and Transport Minister.

---

*Elisabeth Bridge (Erzsébet-hid) D6(L5)

Buses
5, 7, 7A, 8, 78, 112

The modern Elisabeth Bridge replaces a predecessor built at the turn of the century which, for many years, was the largest arched bridge in the world and which was destroyed in the Second World War.
The modern suspension bridge, built between 1961 and 1964 to plans by Pál Sávoly, is 378 m (413 yd) long and 27·5 m (30 yd) wide.

Emmerich Baths

See Tabán

Engels tér (Engels Square) D5(L/M4)

Underground Station
M1, M2, M3 (Deák tér)

Almost 2 ha (5 acres) in extent Engels tér was once the site of a cemetery and is today the location of the long-distance bus station. In the centre of a lawn stands the Danubius Fountain, designed by Ybl in 1883 and originally set up on Kálvin tér. The figures on the fountain by L. Feszler were overhauled by D. Győri in 1959. They symbolise the Danube and its three largest tributaries, the Drau, the Theiss and the Save.

On the east side of the square is a marble memorial by G. Kiss (1906) commemorating Frau Veres (1815–95), who was outstanding in the field of education for women.

J. Horvay (1929) was the sculptor of the bronze figure of a shepherd playing a pipe, on the north-west side of the square. Of considerable architectural merit are the buildings in the Classical manner at József Attila utca Nos. 1 and 2 and the building by J. Hild at József Attila utca No. 16.

Buses
2, 4, 4A, 6, 15, 16

Eötvös tér

See Roosevelt tér

Eötvös University

See Loránd-Eötvös University

Ernst Museum

See Nagymező utca

Erzsébet-hid

See Elisabeth Bridge

Esztergom (Gran)

Esztergom (Gran) is one of the oldest towns in Hungary. It lies on the terraces of the right bank of the Danube at the place where the river breaks through the Hungarian Central Uplands ("Hungarian Wachau"). The old residence of the Hungarian Princes and Kings has, since 1715, been the seat of the Catholic Prince Archbishop of Hungary.

Esztergom, which has many historic buildings, numbers today about 28,000 inhabitants. Since the end of the Second World War industry (especially engineering) has flourished to become, together with tourism, an important factor in the economy.

The Romans maintained a military camp on the site of the present-day town of Esztergom. From the end of the 10th c. the Hungarian Arpads elevated Esztergom to the position of a Residence, where in 1189 the Hohenstaufen Emperor Frederick I, called Barbarossa, was welcomed. The burgeoning town was destroyed by Mongols in 1241 after which the

Information
Széchenyi tér

Location
60 km (37 miles) north-west of Budapest

Buses
From Engels tér

Boats
From landing-stage at Vigadó tér

History

Hungarian King transferred his residence to Buda. In 1526 after the Battle of Mohács, Esztergom became a frontier fortress of the Turkish kingdom, but in 1683 the Austrians reconquered the town. In 1715 the Residence of a Catholic Archbishop was made the seat of the Prince Archbishop of Hungary. From then on Esztergom had its heyday as a religious centre. The Cathedral of Esztergom, the largest and the most magnificent church in the whole of Hungary, was dedicated in 1856. In connection with this event Franz Liszt conducted his "Gran Festival Mass".

Alsó-sziget (Danube Island)

The Island of Alsó-sziget, which is linked to the mainland by three bridges over the Kis-Duna, has in recent years been developed as a recreational park. Landing-stages, sports grounds, an open-air theatre and the very well-known inn, the Halász-csárda, provide for all kinds of leisure activity.

Location
between the Danube and the
Kis-Duna

Old Church (City Parish Church; Öreg templom)

Built during the 1760s the so-called "Old Church" replaces a 13th c. Franciscan church which had been destroyed by the Turks. The reredos of the High Altar by the Hungarian painter János Vaszary (1867–1937) is exceptionally fine.

Location
Pór Antal tér

Bálint Balassi Museum (Balassi Bálint Múzeum)

This museum, named after Bálint Balassi, the Hungarian poet who fell in battle against the Turks near Esztergom in 1594, houses an interesting collection of archaeological and local historical material. The exhibits illustrate the history of Esztergom and include finds of the Middle Ages and of the Turkish era.

Location
Bajcsy-Zsilinszky út 63

Castle Hill (Vár-hegy)

The Castle Hill (156 m (512 ft)) is probably the oldest place of habitation within the boundaries of Esztergom. A few years ago traces of Roman settlements were uncovered here. Also to be seen are the remains of the medieval king's castle and some ruins of the fortifications of the 14th and 15th c. The cathedral, surrounded by the former houses of the canons and the archiepiscopal seminary, are visible far and wide.

*Cathedral (Fószékesegyház)

Esztergom Cathedral was begun in 1822. Its bold architecture, modelled on the Italian Renaissance, is the work of Paul Kühnel and J. B. Packh. The church was completed in 1856 by J. Hild. During the celebrations of the dedication festival Franz Liszt conducted his "Gran Festival Mass" which had been specially composed for the occasion.

Location
Szent István tér (Vár-hegy)

◄ Esztergom

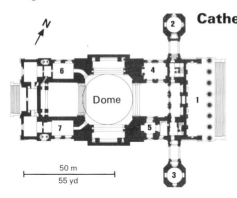

Cathedral of Esztergom
Archiepiscopal
Cathedral Church
Fószékesegyház

1 Entrance Hall

2 North Tower

3 South Tower

4 St Stephen's Chapel

5 Bakócz Chapel

6 Treasury

7 Meeting Hall

50 m

55 yd

Exterior

The exterior of the cathedral is of monumental proportions. The ecclesiastical building is 118 m (387 ft) long and its west front is 40 m (130 ft) wide. Over the crossing rises a dome, 72 m (236 ft) high, borne on twenty-four pillars. Two towers flank the entrance hall which is reminiscent of a Greek temple.

Bakócz Chapel

The most charming part of the interior is the Bakócz Chapel (Bakócz-kápolna), a reconstruction of a chapel commissioned in the first half of the 16th c. by Archbishop and Papal Candidate T. Bakócz. The altar created by A. Ferrucci of Florence is most striking.

Treasury

Numerous exceptionally valuable works of art are kept in the Cathedral Treasury. Of immeasurable value are a Byzantine tablet of the 11th c, a 12th c. Hungarian coronation cross, the "Hill of Calvary" by Matthias Corvinus dating from the 15th c. and various chalices and priestly vestments.

Crypt

In the crypt the magnificently carved tombs of the Archbishops of Esztergom are well worth seeing.

*Archbishop's Palace (Primási palota)

Location
Berényi Zsigmond u.

Opening times
Daily 9 a.m.–5 p.m.

The Palace of the Primate of Hungary was completed in 1882 by the great architect Lippert, in Eclectic style. It contains sacred art brought together by Archbishop J. Simor. Carpets, tapestries and porcelain are also on view, as are works by Italian masters of the 12th to 15th c., among them examples by Lorenzo di Credi, Duccio and Lorenzetti, Hungarian panels, including a "Way of Sorrows" of the first half of the 16th c., an altar and a man's coffin from Garamszentbenedek, probably of the 15th c.

Hotel Fürdő

Location
Bajcsy-Zsilinszky út 14

The baths of Esztergom have been known since Roman days. Adjoining the modern Hotel Fürdő, an imposing Classical building, are thermal indoor and outdoor baths; they occupy the same site as a bath in the 12th c.

Esztergom

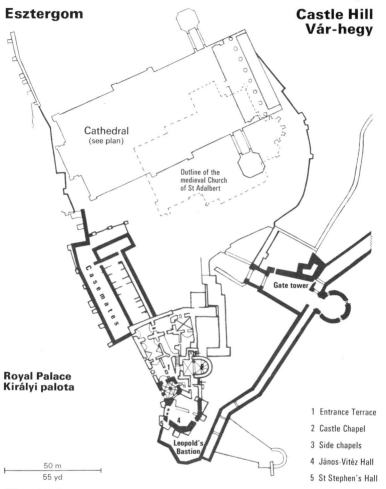

Cathedral
(see plan)

Outline of the
medieval Church
of St Adalbert

Casemates

Gate tower

**Royal Palace
Királyi palota**

1 Entrance Terrace

2 Castle Chapel

3 Side chapels

4 János-Vitéz Hall

5 St Stephen's Hall

Leopold's
Bastion

50 m
55 yd

*Royal Palace (Királyi palota)

The remains of the oldest Hungarian Royal Palace are situated
on the southern promontory of the Castle Hill. They are reputed
to have been erected under Grand Duke Géza in the 10th c.
On the south side of the present cathedral are the remains of St
Adalbert's Church with the Porta Speciosa (red marble).

Passing through a long lapidarium (with some Byzantine
capitals) one reaches a 12th c. tower dwelling. From the room
in which it was reputed King Stephen was born (with red
marble pillars in the centre) one first reaches the widow's

Location
Vár-hegy

Opening times
Daily 9 a.m.–5 p.m.

Tower Dwelling

57

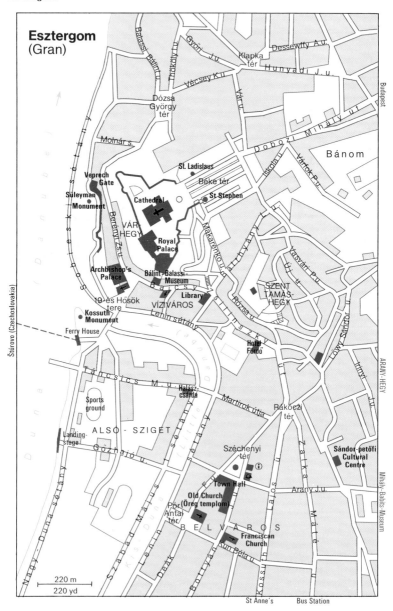

Esztergom
(Gran)

Balassi Bálint u.

Győri J. u.

Dessewffy A. u.

Klapka tér

Hunyadi J. u.

Vécsey K. u.

Vár u.

Dózsa György tér

Molnár s.

Dobozi Mihály út

Budapest

Bánom

Veprech Gate

St. Ladislaus

Béke tér

Süleyman Monument

Cathedral

St Stephen

Bercsényi Zs. u.

VÁR-HEGY

Royal Palace

Iskola u.

Várfok u.

Makarenko u.

Arany J. u.

Tásvári út

Archbishop's Palace

Bálint-Balassi Museum

Bajcsy-Zs.

SZENT TAMÁS-HEGY

19-és Hősök tere

Library

VÍZIVÁROS

Rossa u.

Štúrovo (Czechoslovakia)

Kossuth Monument

Lehin sétány

Ferry House

Lőwy Sándor u.

Táncsics M. u.

Halász-csárda

Hotel Fürdő

Sintér u.

ARANY-HEGY

Sports ground

Martírok útja

Rákóczi tér

Landing-stage

Gőzhajó u.

ALSÓ - SZIGET

Kis-Duna

Little Danube

Nagy - Duna sétány

Széchenyi tér

Sándor-petőfi Cultural Centre

Mihály-Babits Museum

Town Hall

Arany J. u.

Old Church (Öreg templom)

Pór Antal tér

BELVÁROS

Franciscan Church

Zalka Máté

Kossuth Lajos

Szabadság

Deák F.

Bán Béla u.

220 m
220 yd

St Anne's

Bus Station

quarters of Queen Beatrix, the consort of King Matthias, and
then the Hall of Cardinal Virtues with beautiful frescoes of the
school of F. Lippi.

Hall of Cardinal Virtues

The 12th c. Castle Chapel is very impressive; it has a beautiful
rose-window above the stepped doorway where a figure of St
Anna can be seen. The interior contains fragments of medieval
frescoes. On the left is a side chapel probably once the private
chapel of the king or of the archbishop.

Castle Chapel

Mihály Babits Museum (Babits Mihály Múzeum)

On the Elő-hegy which rises to the east of the town can be
found the house of Mihály Babits (1883–1941), an author who
was much read before the Second World War. The house is
now furnished as a memorial to him.

Location
Elő-hegy

St Anne's Church (Szent Anna-templom; Kerek templom = round church)

St Anne's Church was built in the first quarter of the last century
to plans by Johann Baptist Packh. The artist had in his mind the
great model of the Roman Pantheon. His church served as a
model for the new Cathedral of Esztegom.

Location
Hősök tere

St Thomas's Hill (Szent Tamás-hegy)

From St Thomas's Hill, the second noticeable height of the
town, there is a fine view of Esztergom and the Danube.
On the hill stands a chapel dating from 1823. It contains a
notable "Way of the Cross" with 18th c. statues.

Location
East towards the district of
Viziváros

*Széchenyi tér

One of the finest squares in the town is Széchenyi tér which is
surrounded by a number of impressive buildings.
On the south side of the square stands the Town Hall (Városi
tanácsház) which was completed in 1770. House No. 3 (pretty
coat of arms) reveals the influence of the Romantic period; it
was completed in 1862. House No. 7 shows Baroque and
Rococo features. The architecture of houses Nos. 24 and 25 is
in the manner of the second half of the 18th c. (this was known
as "pigtail" style from the fashion of the time when men wore
pigtails).

Location
In the district of Belvaros

---

*Ethnographical Museum (Néprajzi Múzeum)   D4(L3)

The Ethnographical Museum is housed in the former Palace of
Justice, which had been built in 1896 in Neo-Renaissance
style according to the designs of A. Hauszmann.
Over the tympanum, which is borne on six tall columns, can be
seen a troika with the Goddess of Justice by K. Senyei. In the
entrance hall are wonderful frescoes by K. Lotz.
The museum, which was opened in 1872, is primarily devoted
to a collection of Hungarian cultural assets. Part of the

Location
V, Kossuth Lajos tér 12

Underground Station
M2 (Kossuth tér)

Trams
2, 2A

Ethnographical Museum

Parizsi udvar in Felszabadulás tér

Trolleybuses
70, 78

Opening times
Tues.–Sun. 10 a.m.–6 p.m.

extensive Hungarian collection is on show on the first floor. Here articles of rural life, implements for handwork and craft, unusual examples of handicraft and textiles can be seen. Special exhibits are concerned with ethnic groups from Central Asia and Siberia who are related to the Magyars, at least as far as their language is concerned.

On the second floor all the important levels of civilisation and their development are made clear. Of special interest are the New Guinea collection of L. Biró and S. Fenichel, the African collection of S. Teleki and E. Torday and evidence of the culture of the New Stone Age in Central Asia, Siberia, Mongolia, Africa, South America and the Pacific.

Europark

See Buda, Important Streets and Squares, Bécsi kapu tér

Evangelical Church

See Inner Ring, Deák Ferenc tér

Evangelical National Museum

See Inner Ring, Deák Ferenc tér

*Felszabadulás tér (Liberation Square)   D5(M5)

Felszabadulás tér, the busiest square on the southern part of Pest's "shopping centre", has several architectural styles and is one of the most charming squares in the town.
On the side which faces the Danube (see entry) and on both sides of the Szabadsajtó út are two buildings protected by towers, the Klothild Palace and the Mathild Palace, built by K. Giergl and F. Korb in 1902 in Eclectic style.

On the north-west side of the square at the beginning of Kigyó u., which forms part of the recently created pedestrian precinct of Pest, stands the Párizsi udvar, built in the most beautiful Art Nouveau style with elements of Italian and Turkish architecture. At the eastern tip of this complex of buildings, the headquarters of the National Travel Bureau IBUSZ can be found.

See Franciscan Church

Location
District V

Underground Station
M3 (Felszabadulás tér)

Buses
2, 7, 7A, 15, 78, 112

Párizsi udvar

*Ferenc-Hopp Museum of East Asian Art   F4
(Hopp Ferenc Kelet-ázsiai Művészeti Múzeum)

The museum occupies the house of its founder F. Hopp (1833–1919). The collection comprises Japanese, Korean and Indian *objets d'art* (the majority dating from the 16th and 17th c.), including lacquer and bronze work, pictures, carpets, porcelain, jewellery and book illustrations. There is also an archaeological collection.
In the museum garden can be seen selected sculptures from various regions in East and South Asia.
The museum's Chinese collection has been transferred to the China Museum (see entry).

Location
VI, Népköztársaság útja 103

Underground Station
M1 (Kodály körönd)

Buses
1, 4, 4A

Opening times
Tues.–Sun. 10 a.m.–6 p.m.

Ferencvárosi Torna Club

See Népliget

Ferihegy Airport

See Facts and Figures, Transport
See Practical Information, Airport

Fire Brigade Museum

See Kőbánya

**Fishermen's Bastion (Halászbástya)   C4/5(M7)

On Castle Hill, at the place where in the Middle Ages the fishermen had their defence installations, the Fishermen's

Fishermen's Bastion

St Stephen

Location
On the north side of Castle Hill

Buses
16, 16A

Bastion was built behind the Matthias Church (see entry), between 1895 and 1902. Its towers, colonnades and embrasures, which were designed in Neo-Romanesque style by F. Schulek, were recently renovated. From the bastion there is a magnificent panorama over the city.

In the south courtyard of the bastion stands a bronze equestrian statue of St Stephen (Szent István), the first King of Hungary; it is a work of A. Stróbl, dated 1906. In the north courtyard are statues of the monks Julianus and Gellért by K. Antal (1937). From the bastion a double flight of steps leads down to the "watertown" (see Viziváros), past a bronze statue of St George. At the bottom of the steps a memorial to János-Hunyádi, made in bronze in 1905 by István Tóth, can be seen.

Florian Chapel

See Viziváros

Flórian tér

See Obuda

Fortuna utca

See Buda, Important Streets and Squares

Foundry Museum

See Vizivaros

* Franciscan Church (Ferenciek templom)   D5(M5)

The Franciscan Church dominates the north-west side of Felszabadulás tér. This church, which has recently been renovated, dates from the first half of the 18th c. It is built in Baroque style and is the successor to a church which Franciscan monks had founded on this site in the 13th c. In 1541 the Turks turned the church into a mosque.

The façade facing Felszabadulás tér (see entry) is adorned with statues of St Peter of Alcantara, St Francis and St Antony, as well as the arms of the Franciscan Order (over the doorway). On the north-west exterior wall (Kossuth Lajos utca) can be seen a bronze relief by Holló (1905) commemorating Baron Wesselényi, who saved numerous people from drowning in 1838 during a flood. The interior of this single-aisled church has a magnificent High Altar and richly furnished side altars. A special treasure is the wooden pulpit with the Twelve Apostles. On the walls are frescoes and stuccoes by K. Lotz (1895) and V. Tardos-Krenner (1927).

The artists J. Fessl and F. Uhrl (1835) were responsible for the pretty Naiad Fountain outside the church.

Location
V, Felszabadulás tér

Underground Station
M3 (Felszabadulás tér)

Buses
2, 7, 7A, 78, 112

Franz Liszt Academy of Music   E4(N3)
(Liszt Ferenc Zeneművészeti Főiskola)

The Academy of Music established by Franz Liszt (see Notable Personalities) is housed in a prestigious building designed in Secessionist style by the architects F. Korb and K. Giergl between 1904 and 1907. On the main façade is a bronze seated statue of Franz Liszt by A. Stróbl.

In the foyer is a bust of Bartók by A. Beck and a sculpture representing the composer Chopin.

The ground floor occupies two storeys and has room for an audience of up to 1,200; it boasts exceptionally good acoustics. Fine reliefs in the corners of this hall are the work of the artists Groh and Telcs.

The small hall on the first floor is less elaborately furnished. In its foyer is a wall-painting by J. Zichy which symbolises some of the stages in the development of Hungarian music.

The Franz Liszt Academy of Music is now a cultural institution known far beyond the boundaries of Hungary. After Franz Liszt, such well-known musicians as Béla Bartók and Zoltán Kodály worked here (see Notable Personalities), as well as Ernő Dohnányi and Leo Weiner.

The Academy has probably the most important collection of Hungarian musical literature.

Location
VI, Liszt Ferenc tér

Underground Station
M1 (November 7 tér)

Trams
4, 6

Trolleybuses
70, 78

Buses
12, 12A

View from Gellért Hill of the south of Budapest

Freedom Bridge (Szabadság-hid) D6(M5/6)

Trams
47, 49

Bus
1

The steel Freedom Bridge, which links Gellért tér on the Buda bank of the Danube with Dimitrov tér on the Pest side, was opened to traffic in 1896. The plans were by J. Feketeházy. The bridge, which is 331 m (362 yd) long and 20 m (22 yd) wide was destroyed in the Second World War but was the first bridge to be rebuilt, and it was reopened to traffic in 1946.

Freedom Square

See Szabadság tér

Gellért Hill (Gellért-hegy) C/D6(K/L5/6)

Location
Districts I and XI

Bus
27

Probably the most striking feature of the landscape of the Hungarian capital is the panoramic Gellért Hill (235 m (771 ft)): a block of dolomite, the east flank of which falls steeply down to the Danube, the west side consists of terraces which were formerly vineyards. Along its geological fault several medicinal springs emerge which supply the Gellért Baths, Rudas Baths (see Practical Information, Spa Establishments) and the Raizen Baths. The hill is named after Bishop Gellért (see Notable Personalities) who did good works during the time of King Stephen I. According to legend this monk died as

Gellért Monument

Liberation Monument

a martyr in 1046 on Gellért Hill, which was once thought to be a meeting-place of witches.

*Gellért Monument   D6(L5)

On the north-east slope of Gellért Hill stands a statue of the Bishop, the work of G. Jankovits (1902); it is framed by an imitation antique pillared portico. Below the memorial is a man-made waterfall.

Location
I, near the Buda end of Elisabeth Bridge

*Liberation Monument   D6(L5)

On the south-east point of Gellért Hill is the Liberation Monument, commemorating the victorious Soviet Army in the Second World War; it was designed by the artist Zsigmond Kisfaludy Stróbl (1947).
On the limestone plinth stands a female figure, 14 m (46 ft) high, bearing a palm branch. At the foot of the monument can be seen a bronze statue of a Soviet soldier with the Red Flag, flanked by the symbols of progress and destruction.

Location
I, the south-east point of the hill

Jubilee Park (Jubileumi Park)   C/D6(K/L6)

The Jubilee Park was laid out on the occasion of the ceremonies celebrating the fortieth anniversary of the October Revolution. Charming walks, flower-beds and valuable artistic sculptures, among them "Budapest" by István Kiss, attract many visitors on fine days.

Location
XI, the south-west slope of Gellért Hill

Gellért baths outdoors . . .   *and indoors*

Citadel   C/D6(L5)

Location
I, summit of Gellért Hill

The Citadel, built by the Austrians on the summit of Gellért Hill after 1851 is still in good repair. Parts of the fortifications, more than 200 m (220 yd) long and up to 60 m (65 yd) wide, are open to the public (hotel, folklore restaurant in the casemates, exhibitions and viewing platform).

* * Gellért Hotel and Thermal Baths   D6(L/M6)
(Hotel Gellért Gyögyszallo, Gellértfürdő)

Location
1, Szent Gellért tér

Trams
9, 18, 19, 47, 49

Buses
1, 7, 7A

The famous medicinal baths and hotel complex (see Practical Information, Spa Establishments) is, after its recently completed renovation, one of the finest of its kind in Budapest.
There was a spa here as early as the 13th c., when the thermal waters of Gellért Hill were used for medicinal purposes. According to the chronicler Evliya Çelebi of Istanbul the Turks extended the establishment and converted it into a luxurious spa.
The plans for the hotel, which was built in Secessionist style between 1911 and 1918, were by A. Hegedüs, A. Sebestyén and J. Sterk; today it appears in a new light and many well-known people have stayed here. The therapeutic bathing and treatment facilities have been excellently renovated and modernised since 1983 (covered thermal bath, the roof of which can be opened, bubble bath, Turkish bath, etc.), together with open-air facilities including a thermal bath with wave-making equipment which has been designed according to the most modern technical ideas.

Rudas Baths (Rudas-fürdő)

D6(L5)

At the foot of Gellért Hil, at the Buda end of Elisabeth Bridge, are the Rudas Baths (see Practical Information, Spa Establishments). The thermal springs here were already in use in the Middle Ages; the first bath-house dates from that period. In the 16th c. the Turks extended the installation. The typical domed building with its octagonal main room has been preserved from that time. As well as the steam (Turkish) bath there is a pump-room, where medicinal water from the Juventus and Hungária Springs is available.

Location
I, Döbrentei tér 9

Trams
9, 18, 19

Buses
7, 7A, 86

Geological Institute (Földtani Intézet)

G/H4

The buildings of the Institute (1898–1900) in Secessionist style were the work of Ödön Lechner and are notable for their colourful ceramic decoration. On the roof can be seen a sculpture representing three men bearing the world. In front of the building is a monument by A. Stróbl to the geologist and former Director of the institute, J. Böckh. Inside is a highly interesting geological collection.

Location
XIV, Népstadion út 14

Trolleybus
77

Golden Stag

See Tabán

Gran

See Esztergom

Greek Church

See Petőfi tér

Gresham Palace

See Roosevelt tér

Gül-Baba-Türbe

See Rose Hill

Halászbástya

See Fishermen's Bastion

Millennium Memorial in Heroes' Square

*Heroes' Square (Hősök tere)   F3

Underground Station
M1 (Hősök tere)

Trolleybuses
75, 79

Buses
1, 4, 20, 30, 120

The extensive Heroes' Square at the western edge of Városliget (see entry) forms the crossing-point of Népköztársaság útja and Dózsa György út. Its layout was chiefly the work of the architect Albert Schickedanz who was also largely responsible for the huge buildings of the Museum of Fine Art and the Art Gallery which flank the square.

Millennium Monument

The Millennium Monument (Milleniumi emlékmű) is the dominant feature of the square. The 36 m (118 ft) high column is crowned by a figure of the Archangel Gabriel by György Zala. Round the plinth can be seen a group of horsemen in bronze representing the conquering Prince Arpad and six of his fellow warriors. On either side of the column, colonnades extend in a half circle. Between the individual columns are statues of Hungarian regents. On the corner pillars are works in bronze by György Zala representing Work and Prosperity, Chariots of War, Yolk of Peace and Knowledge and Fame. In front of the Millennium Monument is a memorial to the Unknown Soldier.

Art Gallery
(Műcsarnok)

The splendid building in Classical-Eclectic style, which was completed in 1895, serves as an exhibition gallery for various artists. The architecture, which is embellished with colourful ceramic work, was originated by the great Albert Schickedanz. Round the building is an open-air art exhibition.

Museum of Arts and Crafts

See entry

Hess András tér

See Buda, Important Streets and Squares

Historical Museum

See Castle Palace

Hungarian Academy of Science

See Roosevelt tér

Hungarian National Gallery

See Castle Palace

Hungarian National Museum

See National Museum

HUNGEXPO

See Kőbánya

*Imperial Baths and Luke's Baths   C3
(Csásár-fürdő és Lukács-fürdő)

*Imperial Baths (Csásár-fürdő)   C3

The Imperial Baths are one of the oldest of their kind in Budapest. They originated in a Turkish bathing establishment (Hamam) which was in existence under Sokollu Mustafa Pasa. The octagonal domed main room dates from that period. From 1806 Classical additions were made, and these are at present being renovated.

Location
II, Frankel Leó utca 31

Tram
17

Adjoining the wing facing the Danube (see entry) is the Béla-Komjádi Sports Bath (Komjádi Béla Sportuszoda) which was opened in 1976; this has room for 2,000 spectators, and in good weather the roof can be opened.

Béla-Komjádi
Sports Bath

*Luke's Baths (Lukács-fürdő)   C3

An open-air layout connects the Imperial Baths with Luke's Baths to the south. The latter establishment, which is no less renowned than the former, was extended many times from

Location
II, Frankel Leó utca

69

Imperial Baths

Luke's Baths

Tram
17

1760 onwards. Its pump-room is visited daily by a great number of convalescent patients. Adjoining Luke's Baths is a spa treatment centre which is equally well attended.

Institute of Physiotherapy
and Rheumatology

To the south of Luke's Baths is the world-famous Institute of Physiotherapy and Rheumatology (Reuma és Fizioterápiás Intézet).

Mill Pond

Opposite Luke's Baths lies the Mill Pond (Malom-tó), the water-level of which depends on the flow from the thermal springs in the vicinity. On its northern side is St Stephen's Chapel, designed by J. Hild (1844) which has a notable reredos.

---

*Inner City Parish Church (Belvárosi plébánia-templom)   D5(L/M5)

Location
V Március 15 tér/
Szabad Sajtó út

Trams
2, 2A

Buses
5, 7, 7A, 8, 78, 112

The Inner City Parish Church is the oldest church in Pest (see entry). It stands on the remains of the Roman Castrum Contra Aquincum at the Pest end of Elisabeth Bridge (see entry).
In the 11th c. there was a little church here in which in 1046 Bishop Gellért (see Notable Personalities) was buried. In the 12th c. a semicircular choir was added. At that time the church was already being used by the Royal Family.

History of the Building

Extensive rebuilding in the Gothic manner according to French models took place under King Sigismund. The side chapels were added in the second half of the 15th c. During the Turkish occupation the church functioned as a mosque. On the south-

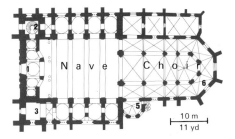

Pest
Inner City
Parish Church
Belvárosi
plébánia-templom

1 Main Doorway   4 Triumphal Arch
2 North Tower   5 Chapel
3 South Tower   6 Former Mihrab

west wall of the choir remains of a Turkish mihrab (niche showing the direction of Mecca) can still be seen. During the siege and the recovery of the neighbouring old royal town of Buda (see entry) by Austrian troops in the years 1684–86, the church was considerably damaged. Years later, rebuilding took place in Baroque style. In 1726 the church received its south tower, in 1735 its new nave and in 1739/40 the north tower. Restoration was undertaken in 1805–08 by J. Hild, and eighty-one years later it was refashioned in Gothic style by the architect Emmerich Steindl. K. Lux worked on the church from 1932 to 1944. In 1948 work began on rebuilding the church which had been severely damaged in the Second World War.

The juxtaposition of two different styles is very impressive. Although the nave and towers have remained in Baroque style the choir reveals the Gothic influence. The main doorway has beautiful statues by Anton Hörger from Buda and on the external wall of the choir is a figure of St Florian also by Hörger.

Exterior

The side altar of John the Baptist (18th c.) is a jewel of art; it was the gift of Proberger, the Burgomaster of Pest. Also notable are the two Renaissance epitaphs in red and pale yellow marble and the pulpit constructed in 1808 by Ph. Ungnad. In the spandrels of the pointed arches in the polygonal south chapel the remains of frescoes can be seen. The modern High Altar was designed by Károly Antal and P. C. Molnár (1948). In the Baptistery is a bronze group by B. Ferenczy (1955).

Interior

---

*Inner Ring (Kiskörút)

D5–E6(L4–M/N5)

The Inner Ring (Bajcsy–Zsilinszky út–Deák Ferenc tér–Tanács körút–Múzeum körút–Kálvin tér–Tolbuhin körút) encircles the old town centre of Pest and follows the former town walls. In recent times Engels tér (see entry) has been included in the Inner Ring.

Locations
District V
Trams
47, 49
Buses:
1, 9

Bajcsy–Zsilinszky út

D4/5(M3/4)

Bajcsy-Zsilinszky út is one of the finest streets in the Hungarian capital. Along it are many buildings in Romantic and Eclectic style.

See entry

Engels tér

Deák Ferenc tér D5(M4)

Underground Station
M1, M2, M3 (Deák tér)

Deák Ferenc tér which adjoins Engels tér (see entry) on the south-east is one of the most important inner-city traffic junctions. Three Underground lines meet here. Of special merit is the Evangelical Church (Evangélikus templom; Lutheran Church) which was built at the beginning of the 19th c. to plans by M. Pollack. The main façade was rebuilt by J. Hild in 1856. The altar is a copy of Raphael's "Transfiguration".

Evangelical National Museum

At present the Evangelical National Museum (Evangélikus Országos Múzeum) is housed in the church and contains very interesting exhibits of church history. Near the church stands the minister's house and the former Evangelical secondary school, both fine Classical buildings.

Underground Museum

The Underground Museum (Földalatti Vasúti Múzeum) occupies a tunnel dug in 1896 for the then first electric Underground railway in Europe. Interesting documents and exhibits, including technical objects, models, drawings, as well as some early carriages, illustrate the development of this mass transport undertaking which was so important for the Hungarian capital.

Tanács körút (Councillors' Ring) D/E5(M4)

In recent years Tanács körút has become an important business street. On its north-east side stands the so-called Madách House (1937), a striking complex of buildings surrounding Madách Imre tér. This is the home of the Madách Studio Theatre. Opposite the Madách House is the exhibition hall of the City Council (No. 4). In the Film Museum (Film Múzeum; No. 3) performances are given, chiefly of meritorious old films.

Múzeum körút (Museum Ring) E5/6(M/N5)

In the Museum Ring two leading Hungarian cultural institutions are located: the National Museum (Nos. 14–16; see entry) and the Neo-Renaissance buildings of the Faculty of Natural Science of Eötvös-Loránd University (see entry), which were designed by Emmerich Steindl. Also of architectural merit is No. 7 for which Ybl was responsible in 1852. In the courtyards of Nos. 17 and 21 remains of the city walls of Pest can still be seen.

National Museum

See entry

Kálvin tér (Calvin Square) E6(N5)

Underground Station
M3 (Kálvin tér)

Kálvin tér, on the southern edge of the centre of Pest, was once known as Széna tér (Hay Market). Today it is an important traffic junction. A few years ago, during building work, remains of the former Kecskeméter Gate of the old city fortification of Pest were discovered here. There are some interesting buildings round the square, including the former inn, The Two Lions (No. 8) dating from 1818. A little aside to the east in Baross tér is the Ervin-Szabó Library (Szabó Ervin Könyvtár) in a 19th c. Neo-Baroque building by A. Meining.

This single-aisled church in a severe Classical style was designed by J. Hofrichter between 1816 and 1859 and built with the co-operation of J. Hild. The four columns of its notable portico bear a tympanum. The interior has a good coffered ceiling and an organ-case designed by Hild. On the left-hand side wall is the funerary monument of Countess Zichy, with a statue by R. Gayard (1854). In the church treasury are valuable articles of goldsmiths' work dating from the 17th, 18th and 19th c.

Reformed Church

Tolbuhin körút (Tolbuhin Ring)   E6(M5)

Tolbuhin körút has in recent years become a busy shopping street, due chiefly to the proximity of the Central Market Hall (see Dimitrov tér). One of the finest buildings in Tolbuhin Ring is No. 12, a fine example of the Classical style. There is a beautiful figure of a dancer in its courtyard.

Institute of Physiotherapy and Rheumatology

See Imperial Baths and Luke's Baths

Jewish Museum

See Pest Synagogue

*Joseph Town Parish Church (Józsefvárosi plébánia-templom)   F6

The imposing Joseph Town Parish Church with its twin towers was built at the end of the 18th c. in Late Baroque style according to plans by J. Thalherr. Since then it has been altered on several occasions. Fine examples of ecclesiastical art are the High Altar by József Hild and the reredos, the "Apotheosis of St Joseph" by the famous Viennese painter Leopold Kupel-wieser. On the façade, between the two towers, a statue of St Joseph by L. Dunaiszky can be seen.

In front of the church stands a monument by Péter Pázmány (see Notable Personalities) to the Bishop of Esztergom and founder of the University of Tyrnau, the precursor of the University of Budapest.

On the other side of Baross útca lies Norváth Mihály tér, named after the Catholic Bishop and Minister of Culture of 1849. His memorial was the work of A. Domján in 1948.

Location
VIII, Baross útca/
Horváth Mihály tér

Trolleybus
83

Buses
9, 17

József Nádor tér (Archduke Joseph Square)   D5(L4)

The square commemorates Archduke Joseph of Habsburg who was elected Palatine of Hungary (the King's deputy) in 1796 and who did a great deal for Budapest. Johann Halbig created his monument in 1859.

The buildings round the square still retain something of the

Location
District V

Underground Station
M1 (Vörösmarty tér)

atmosphere of the last century. This is especially true of No. 1 (1825), built by J. Hild, the outstanding representative of Hungarian Classicism, No. 5 (1859), which was designed according to the ideas of the great Romantic architect H. Máltás, and No. 7, built in Classical style in 1833 by L. Zofahl. Near by stands the very modern administration building of the Ministry of Finance (Pénzügy-minisztérium).

Jubilee Park

See Gellért Hill

Kálvin tér

See Inner Ring

Kapisztrán tér

See Buda, Important Streets and Squares

Kápolna

See Kőbánya

Karl Marx University

See Dimitrov tér

Károlyi Palace

See Petőfi Museum

Kerepesi Cemetery (Kerepesi temető; Pantheon Cemetery)   F–H5/6

Location
VIII, Mező Imre út

Trams
23, 24, 29, 36, 37

Bus
33

The Kerepesi Cemetery is one of the largest in the Hungarian capital. Since the 1950s it has been a cemetery of honour in which notable people are buried.

The Munkásmozgalmi Pantheon (Pantheon of the Workers' Movement) is a monumental building erected by József Körner, with artistic details by Zoltán Kiss.

The mausoleums of Lajos Kossuth, Lajos Batthyány and Ferenc Deák (for all three see Notable Personalities) have places of honour; they were designed by Gerstl and Stróbl, Schickedanz and Gerstner respectively.

King's Bath

See Viziváros

Kiscelli Museum

See Obuda

Kiskörút

See Inner Ring

Kispest (Little Pest)   J/K8

Kispest has only existed since 1871 and is now part of District
XIX. It is the headquarters of large industrial concerns,
including the Red Star engineering works, the Ganz industrial
combine and the Red October textile undertaking. Of particular
interest from the town-planning point of view is the so-called
"Wekerle Settlement" which was methodically laid out on a
chess-board pattern between 1908 and 1925. It comprises
more than 1,000 dwellings.

Station
Kóbánya-Kispest

Underground Station
M3 (Kóbánya-Kispest)

Kóbánya   J/K6–8

Kóbánya (= quarry) forms District X of Budapest. Its name
indicates that until late into the last century, building stone was
quarried here. In the lengthy tunnels various beers are now
stored and mushrooms grown.
In the centre of Kóbánya stands the Church of St Ladislaus
(Szent László-templon) which was built at the turn of the
century from plans of Ödön Lechner. The architecture
combines elements of Neo-Gothic and Secessionist styles.
There is fine Zsolnay ceramic work on the altars and on the
pulpit.

Station
Kóbánya-felsó
Kóbánya-Kispest

Trams
13, 28, 29, 36, 37

Buses
9, 17, 32, 51, 62, 85, 95,
100, 117, 132, 168, 185

Rottenbill Park is named after a former Burgomaster of Pest.
Zoltán O. Kiss created the impressive granite statue of Don
Quixote.

Rottenbill Park

The Greek-Catholic Trinity Chapel (Kápolna) is one of the
oldest buildings in Kóbánya. This Baroque church dates from
about 1740 and has a very fine Baroque altar.

Kápolna

The Budapest Fire Brigade Museum (Tűzoltómúzeum) contains not only documents about the history of the fire brigade
but also a collection of rare historic apparatus.

Fire Brigade Museum

HUNGEXPO   I–K5/6

The Budapest exhibition grounds are situated in the north of

Kodály House

Tram
29

Bus
100

Kőbánya. International fairs are held here every year (May and September/October) and there is also a tourism exhibition which is well attended. Every five years one of the largest agricultural shows of eastern Europe takes place here.

Kodály House

See Népköztársaság útja

Kodály körönd

See Népköztársaság útja

* Kossuth Lajos tér   D4(L3)

Location
District V

Underground Station
M2 (Kossuth tér)

Kossuth Lajos tér is probably the most impressive square in the Hungarian capital. It is surrounded by monumental buildings. On the west side stands the Parliament Building and on the east side the Ethnographical Museum (see entries), the Ministry of Agriculture and Food (Mezőgazdasági és Elemezésügyi Minisztérium; 1885; architect: G. Bukovics) which is in Neo-Classical style. In front of this last-named building are two figures by A. Somogyi.

The south side of Kossuth Lajos is bordered by the very modern

Kossuth Monument

Hungarian Chamber of Trade, which dates from 1972.
On the northern lawns of the square is a monument commemorating Lajos Kossuth (see Notable Personalities) by Zsigmond Kisfaludy Stróbl (1952); on the southern lawn is an equestrian statue of Count Ferenc Rákóczi II by János Pásztor (1935).

Trolleybuses
70, 78

Near Kossuth Lajos tér can be seen the Ministry of External Trade (Külkereskedelmi Minisztérium; Honvéd utca 13–15) and the Ministry of Defence (Honvédelmi Minisztérium, Honvéd utca 26–30). The last-named ministry is housed in a Classical building designed by J. Hild (1839); formerly this building was occupied by the most important silk factory in Pest.

Ministries

Kossuth Lajos utca

D/E5(M4/5)

Kossuth Lajos utca, one of the busiest streets in the Hungarian metropolis leads from Felszabadulás tér (see entry) to the Inner Ring (see entry). On both sides are shops, stores and inns.
At the north-east end of the street (near the Hotel Astoria) the medieval Hatvan town gate which was originally protected by a bastion stood, until well into the 18th c.

Location
District V

Buses
7, 7A, 78

Kun Béla tér

See Üllői út

** Lake Balaton

Lake Balaton (105 m (345 ft) above sea-level), which together with the surrounding area is the most important tourist region in Hungary, attracts more than 600,000 holiday-makers from far and wide every year. The high season lasts from July to September. The lake, which extends from south-west to north-east is 78 km (45 miles) long and up to 14 km (9 miles) wide. It was formed at the end of the Pleistocene period by tectonic sinking of the land. The lake is fed principally by the River Zala and the karst springs in the vicinity of Tapolca. The "Hungarian Sea", as it is called, occupies an area of over 591 sq. km (228 sq. miles) and is, therefore, the largest lake of central Europe. However, twice in the course of its existence it has dried up, owing to its relatively shallow depth (average 3–4 m (10–13 ft); deepest place 12 m (39 ft)) and the corresponding relatively small amount of water that it contains (about 1·8 billion cu. m (2·4 billion cu. yd).

Location
95–190 km (59–118 miles) south west of Budapest

Access
By rail from Budapest Déli pu (South Station)
By car from Budapest via Motorway M 7 (E 96)

Buses
From Engels tér

The shallow Lake Balaton, which has frozen over on several occasions in winter, quickly warms up in summer. The surface temperature can reach 28 °C (82 °F). This and the configuration of the banks – the south bank is very flat and sandy, the north bank more sloping and with pretty bays – provide the best conditions for bathing and water-sports.
The north bank of the lake, the landscape of which is

General

Lake Balaton

Bathing in Lake Balaton

characterised by the foothills of the Bakony range and by evidence of volcanic action in the Pliocene Age, is everywhere delightful and is often called "the Hungarian Riviera". In the south-west, where the Zala joins Lake Balaton, lies Little Balaton (Kis-Balaton), an area which was originally boggy but the greater part of which has now been drained.

North Bank (sights in alphabetical order)

Abrahám-hegy (Abraham's Hill)
Abraham's Hill is, with Badacsony the most celebrated vineyard on Lake Balaton. Monastery ruins.

Alsóörs
Alsóörs is in a charming situation on a terrace on the shore of the lake. Little harbour. Bathing beach. Above the village is the viewpoint Szabadság (296 m (971 ft)).

Badacsony
Well known for its wines, Badacsony (438 m (1438 ft)) is a hill which bears evidence of volcanic action in the Pliocene era. From it fine views may be enjoyed. There are imposing columns of basalt on the summit and slopes. Vines have been grown here for about 2,000 years. Sándor-Kisfaludy House (1772–1844, writer), József-Egry studio (1883–1951, the "painter of Balaton"). There are popular wine festivals in Badacsony and district in autumn.

Balatonalmádi
Balatonalmádi is a resort at the north-east tip of the lake with one of the largest bathing beaches.

Balatonfüred
Balatonfüred, now a much-frequented holiday and spa centre, is the oldest resort on Lake Balaton. It has an establishment

Héviz, lake fed by hot springs

treating heart conditions (carbonic acid mineral spring; see Practical Information, Spa Establishments). First Hungarian yacht harbour. Pump-room. Attractive lake promenade.Mór-Jókai Museum. Beautiful walks. Course for water-skiing with a towing cable 1200 m (1313 yd) long.

Balatonfüzfő is an industrial town, as well as a tourist resort.   Balatonfüzfő

Balatongyörök lies on the southern declivity of the Keszthelyi-hegység. There are wildly romantic rocks and grottoes in the vicinity. A popular wine cellar.   Balatongyörök

Balatonkenese, an ancient settlement on the east bank of Lake Balaton has a church dating from 1606. At the north-west edge of the village can be seen loess caves which were once inhabited. Modern recreational centre by the lake.   Balatonkenese

Balatonrendes is known for its wine. Bathing beach; Bajcsy-Zsilinszky House.   Balatonrendes

From the resort of Balatonszepezd there are opportunities for pleasant walks. Gothic church (13th c.).   Balatonszepezd

There was a settlement here in Roman times. There are interesting tombstones (in the form of a heart) in the churchyard. Near by is the holiday estate of Kilián-telep.   Balatonudvari

The volcanic hill of Csobánc (376 m (1234 ft); basalt summit) lies at the end of the Tapolca Basin. Ruined 13th c. castle. At the south-west foot of the mountain is the "Rossztemplom, a subterranean church built in the 13th c.   Csobánc

Lake Balaton

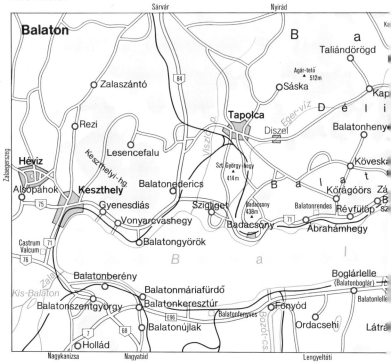

Csopak

Csopak is a romantic vine-growing village. Ranold Castle and the Church of Kövesd are worth seeing.

Dörgicse

There is a medieval look to Dörgicse which is in a beautiful situation. From Halom-hegy (399 m (1310 ft)) there are magnificent views.

Felsöörs

Of interest here is the Romanesque Protestant church dating from the 13th c.

Gyenesdiás

In the vicinity of the resort of Gyenesdiás are wine cellars full of atmosphere. Ilona Chapel. Starting-point for expeditions in the Keszthelyi-hegység.

Hévíz

The health resort of Hévíz (see Practical Information, Spa Establishments), 6 km (4 miles) west of Lake Balaton, has become known for its thermal lake which probably was formed during the last Ice Age. The temperature of the water, which has a sulphur content, is 37 °C (98 °F); the area extends over 47,500 sq. m (5,681 sq yd); the water produced amounts to 30,000 lt (6600 gal.) per minute; the mud at the bottom is slightly radioactive. There are numerous medical and convalescent homes. Beautiful promenades and walks.

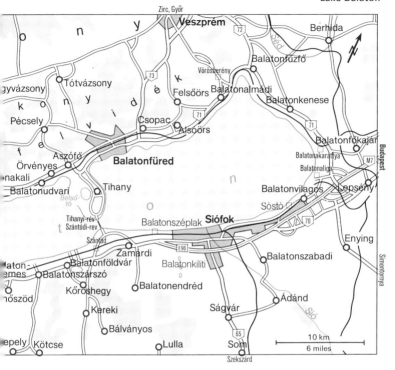

From 1739 Keszthely has been the residence of the Festetics (imposing Baroque castle) and birthplace of the composer Karoly Goldmark. It lies on the west bank of Lake Balaton and is a popular excursion venue. The Georgikon (1797), the first agricultural school in Europe, was the forerunner of the modern high school for agrarian science. Helikon Library, Balaton Museum, Gothic church 14th c.). In summer the Helikon Festival in the park of the Baroque castle. Near the town are the remains of the Roman settlement of Valcum and of Zalavár the ducal seat of the Slavs.

Keszthely

Nagyvázsony has become known because of the 15th c. Kinizsi Castle which was once an important frontier fortress. Open-air ethnographical museum; monastery; Pauline monastery; in summer equestrian games.

Nagyvázsony

Szent György-hegy (414 m (1359 ft)) provides probably the most impressive evidence of Pliocene volcanic activity in the area of Lake Balaton. On the southern slope its basaltic covering is split into columns 30–40 m (100–130 ft) high. Excellent vineyards. Many wine cellars.

Szent György-hegy

Of interest here are the remains of a 13th c. castle and the Avasi

Sziliget

81

Church of the same period, as well as the former Puthéani Castle (18th c. Baroque), once owned by the Eszterhazy family. Bathing beach.

Tapolca

The thriving industrial town of Tapolca (10 km (6 miles) north of the lake; bauxite workings in the vicinity) was once well known for its wine trade. A grotto with a pool is popular; this is part of an extensive system of karst caves.

Tihany

The peninsula of Tihany is the most beautiful holiday resort on Lake Balaton. Luxurious hotels, little harbours for sailing-boats, places of recreation well equipped by the State, and other charming holiday homes give Tihany something of an exclusive character. In addition to the Biological Research Institute of the Hungarian Academy of Science and a branch of the Geophysical Institute, two other important research establishments are located in Tihany.

The only car-ferry across Lake Balaton plies between Tihany and Szantod on the southern shore.

The Tihany Peninsula, the higher parts of which are covered with basalt tufa, was the scene of volcanic activity in Late Tertiary and Quarternary times. It was then that a number of geysers broke through the hard tufa and formed the so-called "geyser humps". Later the central part of the peninsula sank and in the deepest place a sheet of water appeared, not unlike a crater lake. There are traces of a fortification, known as an "ovar", dating from early historical times, and this was later also utilised by the Slavs. Nothing is left of a fortification built after the attacks by the Mongols.

In 1055 King Andrew (Endre) I built the Benedictine Abbey of Tihany which now attracts many visitors. This religious foundation was extended in the 18th c. (monastery buildings and a beautiful Baroque church). Only the crypt of the original abbey church remains today.

The whole of Tihany is now a protected area. Part of it has been set up as an open-air ethnographical museum. In the vicinity are sweet-smelling lavender fields.

Zánka

Zánka is the largest vacation centre on Lake Balaton.

Zalaszántó

Zalaszántó has been inhabited for a very long time (finds of the Ice Age); it is situated on the northern side of Keszthely-hegység. The 13th c. church and castle ruins of the same date are worth seeing.

South Bank (sights in alphabetical order)

Balatonberény

In the old village of Balatonberény well-preserved and architecturally interesting old farmhouses and the 17th c. Fortress of Csillagvár are to be seen.

Balatonboglár

Balatonboglár is one of the oldest holiday resorts on the south shore of Lake Balaton. Near the little village of Buzsák, which is noted for its folk-art (especially costumes), the ruins of the 11th c. Benedictine Abbey of Somogyvár can be seen.

Balatonfenyves

From the resort of Balatonfenyves a narrow-gauge railway runs to Csiszta-puszta (medicinal baths).

Balatonföldvár

Balatonföldvár can look back on a long tradition as a summer

resort. Extensive bathing beach; near by in Zala the house of
Mihály Zichy (1827–1906) the Court Painter of the Russian
Tsarist family.

Balatonlelle is very popular as an elegant holiday resort.

Balatonlelle

In Balatonszárszó, a rather quiet resort, the Attila-József
Museum is worth seeing. The poet died here. A 13th c. church.

Balatonszárszó

Balatonszemes is growing quickly. The 15th c. church with a
valuable reredos, the postal museum (documents, old wagons)
and the "Owl Castle" (Bagolyvár) are among the attractions.

Balatonszemes

Fonyód, the second largest resort on the southern shore of Lake
Balaton, extends along the foot of Vár-hegy (233 m (765 ft)),
which was inhabited in prehistoric times. There are a harbour
and remains of a medieval castle.

Fonyód

Siófok, the largest place and the regional centre of the southern
part of the area of Lake Balaton, has developed in recent years
to become the most popular holiday resort on the lake. The
increase in tourism is largely due to the building of the railway
from Budapest to Fiume. The first baths were opened here in
1866.
Siófok, lies on the little River Sió, a fact which led the Romans
to construct a canal here. It is the birthplace of the operetta
composer Emmerich Kálmán. The Turks, who had established
themselves in a 16th c. moated castle, controlled from here the
entire area to the south of the lake. In 1863 the Sió Canal was
extended at considerable cost.
There is a great deal of information on regional history to be
found in the József-Beszédes Museum (history of the town,
boating on Lake Balaton, building of the Sió Canal, an
Emmerich Kálmán room).
Near Siófok are the remains of the Roman settlement of
Tricciana.

Siófok

Szántod is the terminus of the ferry to Tihany. Ferry-house and
farmhouse (agricultural museum with 18th and 19th c.
implements).

Szántod

The holiday resort of Zamárdi lies on the triangular spit on the
south side of Lake Balaton.

Zamárdi

Léanyfalu

See Szentendre

Lenin körút

See Outer Ring

Liberation Monument

See Gellért Hill

View of Margaret Island

Liberation Square

See Felszabadulás tér

Loránd-Eötvös University   D/E6(M5)
(Eötvös Loránd Tudományegyetem)

Location
V, Egyetem tér 1–3

Bus
15

The central buildings of the Loránd-Eötvös University were erected at the end of the 19th c. in Neo-Baroque style to plans by Herczeg and Baumgarten. As well as the administrative headquarters of this university, which was founded in 1635 by Archbishop Peter Pázmány of Esztergom originally in Tyrnau, the buildings also house the faculty of law and political science.

Luke's Baths

See Imperial Baths and Luke's Baths

Madách Theatre

See Outer Ring, Lenin körút

Marcius 15 tér (Square of 15 March)   D5/6(L5)

The Square at the Pest end of Elisabeth Bridge commemorates in its name the outbreak of the Revolution of 1848.
Here the Romans had set up their Castrum Contra Aquincum, an advanced defence base, the purpose of which was to guard the Danube crossing. The remains of this fortification and documents illustrating its history can be seen in the lower part of the square. I. Tar was the sculptor of the "Legionaries' Fountain" (figures representing Roman legionaries) which dates from 1970.

On the south-west side of the square is the lively inn, Mátyás pince (Matthias Cellar).

See entry

Location
District V

Trams
2, 2A

Buses
2, 5, 7, 7A, 8, 15, 78, 112

Contra Aquincum

° Matthias Cellar

Inner City Parish Church

Margaret Island (Margit-sziget)   C/D1–3

Margaret Island, barely 2·5 km (1·5 miles) long and up to 0·5 km (550 yd) wide, is undoubtedly the local recreation and recuperative centre for the people of Budapest. Thermal springs, feeding the medicinal and swimming-baths, space for sports and games, carefully tended gardens and paths, and not least the remains of buildings which play a significant part in the history of the town daily attract many visitors.

The Romans utilised the supply of thermal water in the north of the island in the Danube. In the 12th and 13th c. Premonstratensian and Franciscan monks and Dominican nuns built monasteries and a nunnery here. Even the Archbishop of Esztergom and the Order of St John of Jerusalem maintained establishments on the island. At the end of the 18th c. the Habsburg Archduke John, Palatine of Hungary, had the island landscaped. At the end of the 19th c. a thermal bath with a pump-room was built, but in the Second World War this was severely damaged. After the war a modern spa centre was established including the fashionable Hotel Thermal, opened in 1978.

The island gets its name from the canonised Princess Margarete (1252–71), the daughter of the Hungarian King Béla IV; because of a vow made by her father she became a nun in the Dominican convent on the island.

In the south of the island stands a metal sculpture by István Kiss (1972) in the form of a flower; it was unveiled on the occasion of the centenary of the union of Obuda, Buda and Pest. On the inside surface of the leaves are symbols depicting the modern history of Budapest.

Near the Union Monument is a large fountain, the waters of which are illuminated on summer evenings.

The Alfréd Hajós Sports Bath (Hajos-Alfréd Sportuszoda) in the west of the island is named after the double Hungarian champion of the first Olympic Games in modern times (1896).

Trams
4, 6, 33V

Buses
C, 12, 12A, 26

History

Name of the Island

*Union Monument

Fountain

Alfréd Hajós Sports Bath

Union Monument . . .   *. . . detail inside the "leaves"*

It was constructed in 1930/31 and includes a covered pool, two open-air pools, a diving-pool and two pools for children. A short distance south is the Pioneer Stadium (Uttörö-stadion).

Franciscan Church (ruins)

Only scant remains have survived of the Church of the Franciscan Monastery which was erected in the 13th/14th c.; these include part of the west side, part of the north wall and of the apse, as well as a fragment of the tower.

*Palatinus Baths

The comprehensive facilities of the Palatinus Baths (Palatinus Strandfürdö) cover an area of 7 ha (17 acres). A bath with artificial waves, together with various medicinal, swimming and children's pools are fed with thermal water and can accommodate up to 20,000 at any one time.

Opposite the Palatinus Baths can be found the pretty Rose Garden (Rózsakert) with a little open-air animal enclosure.

Artists' Promenade

Along the Artists' Promenade (Müvészsétány) can be seen busts of celebrated Hungarian personalities of the art world.

Dominican Nunnery (ruins)

After flooding which occurred in 1838, remains were discovered of the Dominican nunnery which had decayed during the Turkish occupation. The most celebrated nun was Princess Margarete (see above), the daughter of King Béla IV. The convent church was built in the 13th c., rebuilt in the 14th and extended in the 15th. Traces of Romanesque and Gothic architecture have been detected.

Water-tower

Near by stands a 52 m (170 ft) high water-tower (1911) which is at present being converted for tourism purposes. Close by can be found an open-air theatre with room for an audience of 3,500.

Part of the foundations of the 12th c. Premonstratensian monastery are still to be seen. The church of this foundation was rebuilt about fifty years ago in Romanesque style. In the tower hangs a bell, cast in the 15th c., which is one of the oldest in Hungary.

Premonstratensian Monastery

This hotel, completed in 1978, is extremely modern and has become well known far beyond the borders of Hungary. It was designed by the architect G. Kéry and is equipped according to the most recent balneological ideas. Near the hotel can be found an artificial rock garden (sziklakert) with rare plants of much interest.

*Spa Hotel Thermál

The so-called "Musical Fountain" in the north of the island is a copy of one built in 1820 in Tîrgu Mureş in Romania by the Siebenburg specialist P. Bodor. The water-driven mechanism was destroyed in the Second World War.

Musical Fountain

Market Hall

See Dimitrov tér, Central Market Hall

*Martinelli tér — D5(M4)

Martinelli tér was still in use as a market-place in the last century, but today it has become a busy 'turntable" for traffic in Pest.
Of architectural interest is the former Servit Church (Szervíták templom), built in the first half of the 18th c. and rebuilt in the 19th. Its Baroque interior is very fine.

Location
District V

Underground Station
M3 (Deák tér)

Buses
2, 15

The Béla-Lajta House (Lajta Béla-ház; No. 5) dates from 1912 and has recently been made a protected monument. Particularly attractive features of that period are the "hyper-modern" glass façade and the pretty ceramic decoration.

Béla-Lajta House

Just north of Martinelli tér lies Biermann István tér with a beautiful Danaid Fountain by F. Sidló (1933).

Biermann István tér

Marx tér

See Outer Ring

Matthias Cellar

See Marcius 15 tér

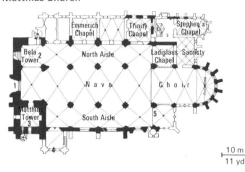

Matthias Church
(Church of Our Lady)
Mátyás-templom

1 Main Doorway

2 Baptistery

3 Loreto Chapel

4 Mary Door

5 Entrance to
Church Museum

**Matthias Church   C5(M7)
(Mátyás-templom; Church of Our Lady, Coronation Church)

Location
Szentháromsáh tér

Buses
16, 16A

Matthias Church

Interior

The Church of Our Lady in Buda is one of the principal sights of the Hungarian capital. It is the successor to a church built in the time of King Béla IV (13th c.), which was rebuilt on several occasions. Its polygon side aisles date from the 14th c. as does the south doorway with its magnificent relief in the tympanum of the "Death of Mary". Side chapels were added in the 15th c. and an Oratory for the Royal Family and a new south tower, which bears the arms of Matthias Corvinus, dated 1470 (the original which gives the church its name is now to be found in the interior). In 1526 the church was destroyed by fire and fifteen years later was converted into a Mosque. After the Turks were driven out by the Austrians, the Jesuits made themselves responsible for the Church of Our Lady and a few years later it became the Coronation Church of the Hungarian kings. It was rebuilt in its present form between 1874 and 1896 by F. Schulek who adopted the Gothic style. At the end of the Second World War the church was severely damaged but was faithfully restored after years of work.

A facsimile of the coat of arms of King Matthias which bears a raven, can be seen on the tower which is 80 m (263 ft) high, square at the bottom but octagonal from the second storey.

The richly ornamented south-west front is flanked by the little Béla Tower and the tall Matthias Tower. Above the doorway in the tympanum is a relief by Lajos Lontai (1890) in coloured granite showing the Madonna with two angels. Above this can be seen a fine rose-window.

A jewel of the varied south side of the church is the Mary Doorway which adjoins the Matthias Tower and opens into a portico. The fine relief in the tympanum representing the Death of Mary was created in the 14th c. On either side of the entrance are statues of King Stephen I (the Holy) and King Ladislaus I (the Holy).

The Interior of the Church of Our Lady in Buda is decorated with geometrical designs and plant ornamentation, reminiscent of the painting in a mosque. The stained glass, some of which illustrates legends of saints of the tribe of Arpad, was made in the last century to designs by B. Székely and K. Lotz. The design of the High Altar is by F. Schulek in the Neo-Gothic style.

The Loreto Chapel is situated in the church tower. It has a black Baroque Madonna on the winged altar and the original of the arms of Matthias Corvinus, dating from the year 1470.

Loreto Chapel

The Baptistery in the Béla Tower still has medieval pillars and capitals. K. Lotz painted the frescoes.

Baptistery

The chapel on the north of the choir is dedicated to St Ladislaus. Beautiful frescoes by K. Lotz illustrate scenes from the legend of Ladislaus.

Ladislaus Chapel

Behind a grill enclosing the Chapel of the Holy Trinity in the north aisle can be seen the sarcophagi of King Béla III and his wife; they were originally buried in the Cathedral at Székesfehérvár and were reinterred in the Matthias Church in 1848.

Chapel of the Holy Trinity

A reredos by Mihály Zichy (about 1890) adorns the chapel dedicated to St Emmerich.

Emmerich Chapel

The crypt, the Oratory of the Knights of St John, St Stephen's Chapel near the Sacristy, and the Royal Oratory now serve as the church museum. In the Royal Oratory, the standards which were raised at the Coronation of King Charles IV and Queen Zita on 30 December 1916 still hang. In the museum are reliquaries, chasubles and other ecclesiastical treasures, and a replica of the Hungarian royal crown.

Church Museum

Millennium Monument

See Heroes' Square

Mill Pond

See Imperial Baths and Luke's Baths

Moszkva tér (Moscow Square)   B4(K/L6)

The triangular Moszkva tér (Moscow Square) is one of the most important traffic hubs of the inner city. The square is dominated by the brick building topped with a crown, which houses the postal administration. The fan-like roof of the Underground station is also a prominent feature.

Location
Disctrict XII

Underground Station
M2 (Moszkva tér)

To the north-east is Széna tér (Hay Square) with the former shooting range, built in 1826, and remains of the medieval fortifications of the town.

Széna tér

Municipal Circus

See City Woodland Park

Municipal Council (Fővárosi Tanács)   D5(M4)

Location
V, Városház utca 9–11

Underground Station
M1, M2, M3 (Deák tér)

Trams
47, 49

Buses
1, 9

A Baroque building, which is now the home of the Municipal Council of Budapest (picture see p. 8), was built between 1716 and 1728 to designs of Anton Erhard Martinelli. Its first use was as a home for those wounded in the Austro-Turkish campaign. Above the gates of the main façade are two fine reliefs, commemorating the Emperor Charles IV (Hungarian King Karl III) and Prince Eugene of Savoy.

In the south entrance gateway (from Kossuth Lajos utca) can be seen a "Pallas Athene" by Adami (1785), which once adorned the fountain outside the Matthias Church (see entry). At the south end of the complex a relief by M. Kovács (1949) commemorating the rebuilding after the Second World War can be seen.

On the southern forecourt stands an aluminium monument by the artist B. Szabados in memory of the first Mayor of the newly formed City of Budapest in 1873.

District Council of Pest

The 19th c. building with three inner courtyards (Városház utca 7), near the City Hall, is now the seat of the District Council of Pest. Of particular architectural interest is the Classical wing, constructed to plans by Matthias Zitterbarth, Junior.

In the first courtyard, which is surrounded by arcades, a beautiful 19th c. wrought-iron fountain can be seen and a memorial tablet honouring the freedom fighters of 1848/49 and the victims of the Uprising of 1956.

Municipal Farm

See Városmajor

*Museum of Applied Arts (Iparművészeti Múzeum)   E6(N6)

Location
IX, Ulloi ut 33–37

Underground Station
M3 (Ferenc körút)

Trams
4, 6

Buses
12, 12A, 182

The Budapest Museum of Applied Arts, one of the oldest of its kind in Europe, dates from 1872; it is housed in a three-storey building which was erected between 1893 and 1896 to the design of Ödön Lechner and Gyula Pártos. The building was extensively damaged during the Second World War and rebuilt in the 1950s. With its domed projecting range it is an outstanding example of Oriental-Hungarian Secessionist style. The red granite facing of the exterior (prepared in the Zsolnay porcelain factory of Pćs) and the ceramic work which beautifies the roofs and corners is particularly fine.

Opening times from Tuesday to Sunday, 10 a.m. to 6 p.m.

Furniture

The collection comprises: old Húngarian furnishings, 18th c. French furniture, musical instruments and models.

Textiles

Ecclesiastical vestments and costumes, valuable Coptic weaving (4th–7th c.), Anatolian carpets, Renaissance materials, Dutch Gobelin tapestries, French, Italian and Hungarian lace and various other hand-crafted articles.

Precious metal work

Goldsmith's work (15th–17th c.); articles of silver, bronze, copper and pewter; old Hungarian and Siebenburg jewellery (some of it enamelled); clocks.

Museum of Fine Arts in Hősök tere

Herend porcelain, faience by Holic and Tata, Haban cutlery, ceramics from famous manufacturers.

Glass and ceramics

Carved ivory, pearl ornaments, leatherwork, bookbinding, various fashion accessories.

Small handcrafted articles

Museum of Fine Arts (Szépművészeti Múzeum)   F3

The Budapest Museum of Fine Arts is one of the most important European art museums. Its collection of Italian masters of the Renaissance enjoys an international reputation. The Neo-Classical monumental bulding was completed in 1906 to the designs of Albert Schickedanz and Fülöp Herzog. The portico is very impressive; its huge Corinthian columns bear a tympanum with a relief inspired by one on the gable of the Temple of Zeus in Olympia.
Opening times from Tuesday to Sunday, 10 a.m. to 6 p.m.
There are a number of outstanding works among the very many on display:

Location
XIV, Hősök tere

Underground Station
M1 (Hősök tere)

Trolleybuses
75, 79

Buses
1, 4, 20, 30, 120

Egyptian Department
Mummies and decorated mummy cases, gravestones, statues and statuettes, the remains of a Temple of Ptolemy.

Impressive exhibits

Graeco-Roman Department
Items dating from the 1st, 2nd and 3rd c. BC, among them gold and bronze work and terracotta.

Room 1

Works of art of the 4th and 5th c. BC, including the bronze Grimani jug, vases and an Attic tomb relief.

Room 2

Museum of Fine Arts

Room 3	Etruscan, Roman and Greek exhibits of the 1st c. BC, notably the figure of a dancer and a Tyche statue.
Room 4	Works of art of the Roman era, including the representation of the victory of the Emperor Augustus at Actium and attractive small sculptures.

Renaissance Hall
In the centre of the hall are fine Venetian fountain wreaths. There are wonderful frescoes of the 14th, 15th and 16th c. from various places in Italy.

Department of Modern Sculpture

Room 1	Works by European artists, among them the "Round Dance" by R. Rossi, the "Seated Woman" by Trubetzkoi, the representation entitled "A Mother's Sorrows" by Meštrović and Hildebrand's "Autumn".
Room 2	Works by French artists, including Rodin's "Eternal Spring", "Bronze Age", etc., bronze sculpture by Maillol, Carpeaux's "Spring" and a "Portrait of a Woman" by Despiau.

Graphic Collection
The graphic collection comprises about 10,000 drawings, and some 100,000 engravings. From time to time exhibitions, chosen from this comprehensive stock, are mounted; these deal with particular epochs and schools, or with the works of outstanding artists. The collection includes studies by Leonardo da Vinci as well as drawings by Rembrandt, Manet, Cézanne, Gainsborough and numerous other well-known artists.

Engravings
Examples by Dürer, Rembrandt, Goya and other renowned artists.

Art of the 20th Century
In this collection the works most admired are by Hans Arp, Marc Chagall, György Kepes, Pablo Picasso, Victor Vasarély and Fritz Wotruba.

Old Masters

Room 1	Tuscan painting of the 13th and 14th c. (especially sacred subjects).
Room 2	Tuscan painting of the 14th and 15th c., including work by Giovanni da Ponte and Taddeo di Bartolo.
Room 3	Works of art of the 15th and 16th c. from central Italy, among them examples from the school of Giovanni Santis, as well as works by Domenico and Rodolfo Ghirlandaio.
Room 4	Works of the 14th, 15th and 16th c. from northern Italy, including paintings by Gentile Bellini and Michele Pannonio (an artist of Hungarian origin).
Room 5	North Italian masters of the 16th c., including pictures by Bassano, Giorgione, Sebastiano del Piombo and Veronese.
Room 6	Piedmontese and other North Italian painters of the 15th and 16th c.
Galleries 1, 2 and 3	Italian masters of the 15th, 16th and 17th c., including works by Carracci, Correggio, Francesco Francia, Filippino Lippi and Lorenzo Lotto.
Room 7	Various Italian masters of the 16th and 17th c.
Room 8	Representatives of Italian Baroque painting, among them Bernardo Bellotto, Bernardo Strozzi and Giovanni Battista Tiepolo.

Italian Baroque painters.	Galleries 4 and 5
Dutch masters of the 16th and 17th c., including works by Pieter Bruegel the Elder.	Room 9
Various Dutch masters of the 16th and 17th c., including works by Hans Memling and Jan Bruegel the Elder.	Galleries 6, 7 and 8
Dutch paintings of the 17th c., including Rembrandt's "Old Rabbi" and "The Angel appears to Saint Joseph".	Room 10
Dutch masters of the 17th c.	Room 11
Works by various Dutch masters of the 17th c., among them paintings by Franz Hals, Jan van Goyen and Ruysdael.	Galleries 9–17
Flemish masters of the 17th c., including paintings by Rubens and Van Dyck.	Room 12
Flemish masters of the 17th c. (various artists).	Room 13
Spanish and Portuguese masters of the 15th and 16th c.	Room 14
Spanish masters of the 16th c., including works by El Greco.	Room 15
Spanish masters of the 17th c., including works by Esteban, Murillo and de Ribera.	Room 16
Spanish masters of the 17th c., with works by Goya ("Girl with a Jug", "Portrait of Señora Bermudez", etc.) and Velázquez ("Farmers at Table").	Room 17
German masters of the 15th c., with Hans Holbein's "Death of Mary".	Room 18
Various German painters of the 15th and 16th c., including works by Lucas Cranach, Albrecht Dürer and Hans Baldung Grien.	Room 19
German Baroque painters, including Jan Kupetzky.	Room 20
German and Austrian painters of the 18th c., among them works by Angelika Kauffmann and Franz Anzon Maulbertsch.	Room 21
English masters of the 18th c., including works by Gainsborough, Hogarth and Reynolds.	Room 22
French masters of the 17th and 18th c., among them paintings by Chardin, Lorrain and Poussin.	Room 23

Art of the 19th century
Special attention should be paid here to works by Böcklin, Corot, Courbet, Delacroix, Cézanne, Gauguin, Leibl, Manet, Monet, Pissaro, Renoir, Toulouse-Lautrec and Waldmüller.

Old Sculptures
The majority of the exhibits in this department are works by Italian artists. The *pièce de resistance* of the whole collection is the equestrian statue by Leonardo da Vinci in Room 8. Also noteworthy are Baroque works of art, including those by Georg Raphaël Donner and Johann Christoph Mader.

Museum of the Hungarian Workers' Movement

See Castle Palace

Museum of Military History

See Buda, Important Streets and Squares, Kapisztrán tér

Music Academy

See Franz Liszt Academy of Music

Musical Fountain

See Margaret Island

Museum körút

See Inner Ring

Nagykörút

See Outer Ring

*Nagymező utca (Pest Broadway)   D/E4(M3)

Location
District VI

Trolleybuses
70, 78

Nagymező utca crosses Népköztársaság útja (see entry) near the State Opera (see entry) and for a long time has been known as the Pest Broadway. Its reputation is not only due to the various establishments for night-life, among them the Moulin Rouge (No. 15), but also for the number of theatres in this street. The most important of these are the Municipal Operetta Theatre (Fővárosi Operettszínház; No. 17), the Thália Theatre (Thália-színház; No. 22), the political cabaret Mikroszkóp (No. 24) and the Literary Theatre Miklós Radnóti (No. 11).

Ernst Museum

In the Ernst Museum (No. 8) temporary exhibitions on various fine arts subjects are mounted.

Nagytétény

Station
Nagytétény

Tram
43

Buses
3, 13, 14, 101, 103, 113

Nagytétény is the most southerly part of Budapest (District XXII) on the Buda side of the Danube and is largely an agricultural region. From the 2nd to the 5th c. a Roman military camp was in existence.
In Nagytétény, which was probably named after a Magyar leader, viticulture played a major role from early times but in the last few decades has been gradually losing its former importance.

*Castle Museum (Nagytétény Kastély-múzeum)

Location
Csókási Pál utca 9

Opening times
Tues.–Sun. 10 a.m.–6 p.m.

The most important point of interest in Nagytétény is the Baroque castle which now houses a branch of the Museum of Applied Arts. The great country house ws built in the 18th c. and use was made of remains of 15th c. buildings. It was severely damaged during the Second World War and a few years ago was carefully restored and opened as a museum.

Exhibits

Of interest are finely constructed furniture from the 15th to 19th c. (predominantly of Hungarian and German origin), and a collection of stove tiles and stoves. In some of the rooms are

Façade of the Hungarian National Museum

valuable paintings, carpets, china and clocks, dating from the 18th and 19th c. In the castle stables interesting finds of the Roman Age can be seen.

National Gallery

See Castle Palace

National Library

See Castle Palace, Széchenyi National Library

*National Museum (Magyar Nemzeti Múzeum)   E6(N5)

The National Museum, founded in 1802 by Count Ferenc Széchenyi and includes among its exhibits the Hungarian Royal Regalia, is housed in a large Classical building erected in 1847 to the plans of M. Pollack. The portico of the building is very impressive with Corinthian pillars supporting a triangular gable which is adorned with allegorical figures. In front of the museum stands a monument to the famous Hungarian poet János Arany (1817–82), which was created by A. Stróbl in 1893. In the park-like museum garden other busts and monuments of notable personalities can be seen.
Opening times: Tuesday to Sunday, 10 a.m. to 6 p.m.

Location
VIII, Múzeum körút 14–16

Underground Station
M3 (Kálvin tér)

Trams
47, 49

Buses
1, 9

95

Népköztársaság útja

Ground floor

On the ground floor are many interesting objects dating from pre- and early-historical times as well as from the Roman epoch and the age of the migration of peoples.
Notable among the exhibits in the Department of Pre- and Early-History (rooms I and II) are finds from Vértesszőlős and Sümeg. The *pièce de résistance* of the Bronze Age collection (rooms III and IV) is the Pécel cart. Room V is devoted to the Iron Age. The Roman period comes to life in the entrance hall and in rooms VI, VII and VIII. The complete preserved floor mosaic of the 3rd c B.C. which was found at Veszprém is extremely beautiful and is on show in the foyer of the National Museum. In addition hand-crafted articles (some of them in bronze) and military objects are worth attention.
In the vestibule can be seen valuable evidence from the time of the great migration of peoples, including jewellery of the Huns, a Carolingian sword and utensils of Slav tribes.

First Floor

On the first floor the history of Hungary from the occupation by the Magyars until the year 1849 is depicted.
The most important exhibit of the museum is the Hungarian Royal Regalia, dating from the time of the Emperor Sigismund and of Matthias Corvinus; it includes the crown of the Byzantine Emperor Konstantinos Monomachos, the death crown from Margaret Island. Other gold and silver work of incalculable value is on show in the treasury.
In room III the Renaissance Stallum from Nyíbátor can be seen, as well as Hungarian and Turkish weapons. Mementos of the freedom fight of Prince Ferenc Rákóczi II in the 18th century can be found in room IV, and works of art from the Baroque age as well as mementos of the peasant uprising of the 18th century in room V. Rooms VI and VII are devoted to the 18th and 19th c. and include material and documents of the Hungarian Jacobin movement as well as of the Revolution of 1848/49.

Second Floor

Exhibits from the Science Museum are presented on the second floor. The mineral and rock collections, the special exhibition "Animals of Hungary" and an outline of the evolution of mankind are all very informative.

North Wing

The Széchényi Library with its comprehensive collection (including 2 million volumes and over 350,000 manuscripts) has been transferred to the Castle Palace (wing F) in Buda.

---

*Népköztársaság útja   D–G3–5(M/N3/4)
(Street of the People's Republic; formerly Andrássy út)

Location
District VI

Underground Stations
M1 (Bajcsy-Zsilinszky út–Mexikói út)

Buses
1, 4

The Budapest boulevard Népköztársaság útja which is 2·3 m (1·4 miles) long, was laid out from 1872 and leads in a north-easterly direction from Engels tér (see entry) to Hősök tere (see Heroe's Square). Fine palaces, important cultural buildings (including the State Opera and the Ferenc-Hopp Museum; see entries) and fine old villas line this imposing thoroughfare which since 1896 has been followed by one of the oldest underground railway lines of Europe.

Postal Museum

The Museum of the Hungarian Post Office (Posta Múzeum; No. 3) is housed in an unusual palace, which was designed by C. Czigler in the 1880s. The stairwell is embellished by fine ceiling-paintings by K. Lotz. As well as interesting documents concerning the development of the Hungarian post-office system, the postal history collection has original technical apparatus including the telephone of the Hapsburg Emperor Franz Joseph I and a transmitter of 1919.

Népköztarsaság útja passes the State Opera House (see entry), crosses Pest Broadway (see Nagymező utca) and passes between Jókai tér (monument by A. Stróbl) and the Liszt Ferenc tér with the Franz Liszt Music Academy (see entry).

The first section of Népköztársaság útja with its many Neo-Renaissance buildings ends at the octagonal November 7 tér. Here it crosses the Outer Ring (see entry) and continues as a boulevard on to Kodály körönd. In this stretch the following buildings are worthy of note: the former Academy of Music (No. 67) by A. Lang in Neo-Renaissance style, dating from 1879. This was also the home of Franz Lizst (memorial tablet). | November 7 tér

The State Puppet Theatre (Allami Bábszínház; No. 69) was also built by A. Lang in 1877. On its upper floor are frescoes by K. Lotz. L. Rauscher was the architect in 1875 of the Academy of Fine Art (Kepző muvészeti Foiskola; No. 71) in Neo-Renaissance style. | Puppet Theatre

The Kodály körönd, a beautifully laid-out circular open space is named after the great Hungarian composer (see Notable Personalities). This square is bounded by statues of Hungarian freedom fighters: Vak Bottyán (d. 1709), by G. Kiss Kovács (1958); Miklós Zrinyi (d. 1566), by J. Róna (1902); György Szondi (d. 1552), by L. Marton (1958); and Bálint Balassi (d. 1594) by P. Pátzay (1959). | Kodály körönd

In the last section of Népköztársaság útja can be found at No. 89 the former residence of Zoltan Kodály and a palace (Nos. 88–90), dating from 1882, designed by G. Pertschacher with Neo-Renaissance work on the façade by L. Rauscher and a wrought-iron gate by G. Jungfer. | Kodály House

See entry | Ferenc-Hopp Museum of East-Asian Art

See entry | State Opera

*Népliget (People's Park) H/I6/7

With an area of 112 ha (277 acres), Népliget is the largest park in the Hungarian capital. It was laid out in the 1860s to the south-east of the city centre. On the occasion of the centenary of the union of Obuda, Buda and Pest, Népliget was refurbished according to the latest horticultural ideas. The park with its various monuments, fountains and cascades, flower-beds, greenswards and old stands of timber, is extremely popular. In the north part of the park there is a motor-cycle race-track. **Buses** 55, 99, 182.

Location
District X

Underground Station
M3 (Népliget)

Tram
23

Trolleybus
75

Planetárium

The Planetárium, opened in 1977 in the south-west part of Népliget, is one of the most modern of its kind in eastern Europe. In the dome-room (diameter 23 m (75 ft)) visitors can see an astro-show made possible by the use of Zeiss-Jena projection apparatus.

Ferencvárosi Torna Club (FTC Budapest)

In the north-east corner of Népliget and outside the park to the south-west – on the far side of Üllói út – lies the extensive sports ground of the historic Ferencvárosi Torna Club (FTC), the football section of which has an international reputation.

---

*Népstadion (People's Stadium)   G/H4/5

Location
Népstadion út/Ifjúsag útja/
Verseny útja

Underground Station
M2 (Nepstadion)

Trolleybuses
77, 80

Bus
95

Close to the East Station lies the Budapest 'Sports Town' with the Népstadion (People's Stadium) as its centre. This arena, built in 1953 to the plans of K. Dávid, covers an area of 17,500 sq. m (20,900 sq. yd). Its stands can accommodate more than 70,000 spectators. It is planned to increase the capacity to 100,000 seats.

Along the Ifjúsag útja (Street of Youth), which leads to the stadium, there are notable sculptures on both sides of the road in praise of sport.

Round the stadium are other sporting facilities: the Kisstadion (small stadium; 1962; accommodation 15,000), which has already served as a stage for many show-business artistes; the Millenáris Cycle Race-track (1896), the Nemzeti Sportcsarnok (National Sports Hall (1940)), the Játékcsarnok (Games Hall), the Testnevelési és Sportmúzeum (Museum of Physical Culture and Sport), the Olimpiaicsarnok (Olympia Hall), the Körcsarnok (Circular Hall) and the ultra-modern Uj Sportcsarnok (New Sports Hall (1981), 12,500 seats), which shortly after its completion became in 1983 the venue of the World Gymnastics Championships.

Nép-sziget

See Angyalföld

New City Hall

See Váci utca

November 7 tér

See Népköztársaság útja

---

*Obuda   A–D1/2

Location
District III

HEV line
Batthyány tér–Szentendre

Until its union with Buda and Pest in 1872, Obuda was a somewhat sleepy little town, but in spite of considerable rebuilding and modernisation it has still managed to retain something of its former atmosphere. This old settlement, where evidence of prehistoric culture has been discovered and where shortly after the birth of Christ the Romans founded their camp of Aquincum, was according to tradition the residence of the Hunnish king Attila in the 5th c. Under the Arpads the place experienced enormous prosperity. In the Middle Ages there was a palace of the Hungarian queens here; in the days of the Turkish occupation the little town on the Danube fell into complete decay, due to the increasing importance of the royal city of Buda. Not until the 17th c. was life restored to the town by German-speaking settlers.

Trams
17, 33

Buses
6, 11, 18, 37, 42, 55, 84, 86, 111, 134, 137, 142, 165

Kiscelli Museum

B1

Kiscelli, a part of Obuda, owes its name to a copy of the miracle-working statue of the Virgin Mary of Mariazell. Here there is a branch of the Historical Museum, housed in rooms of the former Trinitarian monastery (18th c.; architect J. Entzenhoffer). The monastery, which acquired the beautiful Baroque gateway in 1910 designed (1799) by F. A. Hillebrandt for the house of the Jesuit Order in Vienna, has quite recently been thoroughly renovated.

Location
Kiscelli utca 108

Bus
165

Documents and objects on show provide a good general impression of the economic and cultural life of the three Danube towns of Buda, Obuda and Pest from the end of the Turkish occupation. Of particular interest are the pictures and accounts of the recovery of Buda by the Austrians in 1686.

Exhibition

Former Synagogue

The former synagogue, which since the Second World War has been used as a cultural centre, was built in the Classical style by A. Landherr between 1820 and 1825. Six pillars and a tympanum with the tablets of the law enhance the main façade.

Location
Lajos utca 16

Obuda Parish Church (Obudai plébánia-templom)

C1

This Baroque church was built in the 1740s to plans by J. G. Paur. Inside and in front of the church can be seen fine figures by K. Bebo.

Location
Lajos utca 17

*Zichy Castle (Zichy-kástély)

D1

Commissioned in the middle of the 18th c. by Count Nicholas Zichy, this Baroque castle (architect J. H. Jäger), was severely damaged during the Second World War and has had a lengthy restoration; for some time it has been used as a cultural centre. It houses a local museum and mementoes of Lajos Kassák (1887–1967), the versatile representative of the Hungarian avant-garde. From time to time excellent concerts are put on here.
Near by, also in Fő tér, are the Town Hall of Obuda and a number of very pleasant inns.

Location
Fő tér 1

Flórian tér (Florian Square)

C1

Flórian tér is an important traffic junction. On its north side can be seen ruins of the baths of the Roman legion (Római katonai fürdő maradványai). The bath itself, the sweat-room and the cold-water pool are well preserved. Adjacent is a small museum (documents about the baths and medicine in Roman times). At the south edge of the square, in the area of Kálvin Köz, are the remains of the medieval queens' palace and the Reformed church of Obuda, which was built in the 18th c.

Filatorigát (former silk-mill)

Location
Harrer Pál utca 44–46

The oval building of the former silk-mill (1785) is now important as an historic industrial building. It commemorates the development of textile production in Obuda which was demanded by the Emperor Joseph II.

Cella trichora (Early Christian graveyard)

Location
Corner of Raktár utca/
Hunor utca

The remains of an Early Christian graveyard, laid out in the second half of the 4th c. on a clover-leaf plan, is known as "cella trichora". In the vicinity are ruins dating from the 1st to the 3rd c. AD.

Villa of Hercules

Location
Meggyfa utca 19–21

In the 1950s and 1960s, the ruins of a magnificent Roman villa (probably dating from the beginning of the 3rd c. AD) were excavated. The mosaics discovered here, which are among the finest which have ever been found in Hungary, depict scenes from the Hercules myth and the Dionysus legend. The sarcophagi exhibited in the garden of the archaeological museum were made in the 3rd and 4th c. AD.

*Roman Military Town (Táborvárosi Múzeum)   C1

Location
Corvin utca 63

In 1950 the remains of the military camp, belonging to the Roman town of Aquincum were discovered to the south of Flórian tér. As well as remains of buildings dating from the 2nd to the 4th c., tools, various vessels and sarcophagi were also found. Also of interest are the remains of a hypocaust.

**Aquincum (plan of excavation see page 102)

Location
Szentendrei út 139

HEV stop: Aquincum v.m.

Buses: 42, 134, 142

The remains of the Roman town of Aquincum, founded in the 1st c. AD on the west bank of the Danube, have been systematically excavated since the 1870s. A considerable part of the former municipality is now accessible as a museum.

History

About the year 10 BC the Romans occupied the territory of their later province of Pannonia. A few years after the birth of Christ they built within the boundaries of Obuda, now a part of Budapest, a military camp, round which a civil town soon arose, which was to reach its heyday in the 2nd and 3rd c. The

Archaeological Museum of Aquincum

flourishing settlement of Aquincum became, as early as the beginning of the 2nd c., the principal town of the province of Pannonia Inferior. The Emperor Septimus Severuss raised it to the status of a "colonia" in AD194.

After the defeat of the Pannonian legions at Hadrianopolis in the year 378 Aquincum declined and the decline was accelerated by increasing and violent attacks by the Barbarians.

In the rooms of the Archaeological Museum, opened in 1894, are exhibited cult objects, sculptures, fragments of mosaics, implements, vessels, coins and jewellery. Among the most valuable exhibits are a water-organ of AD 288, which has become celebrated, a Jupiter column, a marble Diana and a marble Minerva, a statue of Mithras and a written document dated AD 19 (the oldest piece of writing which has until now been found in Hungary); in addition gems and ivory-carving have recently been found.

Archaeological Museum

In the Pillared Hall and in the Lapidarium fine stone-carvings (altars, gravestones, reliefs) can be seen.

Pillared Hall and Lapidarium

The ruins round the museum give an impression of the Roman civil town, some 400 m (440 yd) × 600 m (660 yd) in area, which was laid out according to a plan; as well as numerous and generally one-storeyed private houses it had several large bathing establishments, a market-hall, a Mithras sanctuary and a basilica (probably formerly the "forum").

Ruins in the open

The provision of water and the sewage system (water-pipes, disposal pipes and heating installations) will be of interest – and not only to specialists.

Aquincum

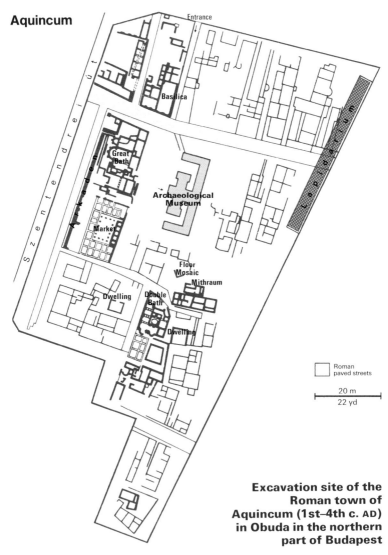

Entrance

Basilica

Great Bath

Archaeological Museum

Market

Floor Mosaic

Mithraum

Dwelling

Double Bath

Dwelling

Lapidarium

Szentendrei út

Arkaden

Roman paved streets

20 m
22 yd

Excavation site of the Roman town of Aquincum (1st–4th c. AD) in Obuda in the northern part of Budapest

*Amphitheatre of the Roman Military Town

Location
Corvin Ottó utca, Corner of Nagyszombat utca

In the 2nd c. AD the Romans built a large amphitheatre for their military camp at Aquincum. Its ruins were excavated in 1940. The arena, constructed on an elliptical plan, was 131 m

(143 yd) long and 107 m (117 yd) broad, and had room for 15,000 spectators who could enjoy war games here, especially those of a circus-like nature.
Some historians have expressed the opinion that the Magyars used this theatre in the 9th and 10th c. when they occupied the country.

Amphitheatre of the Roman Civil Town

In 1880 and 1937 the remains of the amphitheatre of the civil town of Aquincum were excavated. It originally occupied an area of about 80 m (87 yd) × 90 m (98 yd) and accommodated some 7,500 spectators.

Location
Szentendrei utca (near the subway under the railway)

On the opposite side of the road can be seen a restored section of the ancient fortifications of the town.

Opera

See State Opera

Országház

See Parliament Building

Országház utca

See Buda, Important Streets and Squares

*Outer Ring (Nagykörút)   D3–F6(M/N3/4)

The 4 km (2½ mile) long Outer Ring leads from the east end of Margaret Bridge in a half-circle round the city of Pest to the east end of the Petőfi Bridge. It consists of the following sectors: Szent István körút, Marx tér, Lenin körút, November 7 tér, Lenin körút, Blaha Lujza tér, József körút, Ferenc körút, Boráros tér. The ring, which was opened to traffic in 1896 and along which are many imposing buildings dating from the end of the last century, occupies the course of an arm of the Danube which had been filled in, but which in 1867 it was proposed to make navigable for ships.

Trams
4, 6

Buses
12, 12A

Szent István körút (St Stephen's Ring)   D3/4

Szent István körút is the most northerly sector of the Outer Ring. At its west end lie Marx-Engels tér (monument by G. Segesdi, 1971) and Jászai Mari tér, where the Central Committee of the Hungarian Socialist Workers' Party has its headquarters. Further east is the Theatre of Comedy (Vigszínház; No. 14), which in the 1890s was designed by the Viennese architects Fellner and Helmer. The theatre was destroyed in the Second World War but has now been completely rebuilt.

Café Hungária, entrance . . . *and interior*

Marx tér (Marx Square)   D4

Underground Station
M3 (Marx tér)

West Station

Marx tér, which from 1978 was redesigned at considerable expense, is also the forecourt of the West Station (Nyugati pályaudvar), a protected building which was erected in the 1870s by the Parisian firm of Eiffel. The first trains on Hungarian territory were run in 1846 from the site now occupied by the West Station.

Lenin körút (Lenin Ring)   D4–F5(M3–N4)

Palais Batthyány

There are a number of notable buildings along Lenin körút. No. 67 is a copy of the Florentine Palazzo Strozzi, designed by A. Hauszmann in 1884 for Count Batthyány; it is now occupied by a register office.

Hotel Royal

The Hotel Royal (No. 45) was built in the 1890s to plans by the architect Ray. Twenty years ago it was modernised and extended.

Madách Theatre

The Madách Theatre (Madách Szinház; Nos. 29–33) was adapted in 1961 from an existing 19th c. place of entertainment. In this popular theatre can be seen wall-mosaics by the female artist Eszter Mattioni.

*Café Hungária

The Café Hungária (Nos. 9–11) was internationally famous as the Café New York until the Second World War. During the first thirty years of this century, writers, publishers and various well-known personalities used to meet together on the ground floor

The Parliament Building dominates the Danube bank of Pest

of the Palais New York built by A. Hauszmann, K. Giergl and F. Korb between 1891 and 1893. The four-storey building in Neo-Renaissance style was severely damaged during the Second World War but has been restored. The refurbished Café Hungária is much admired, especially by tourists from the West. It is a model of Late Eclectic interior architecture.

Blaha Lujza tér   F5

This square, situated where the Outer Ring crosses Rákóczi út (see entry), is named after the famous Hungarian actress Lujza Blaha (1850–1926) who had great success in the National Theatre which was formerly situated here.

Underground Station
M2 (Blaha Lujza tér)

Palatinus Bathing Beach

See Margaret Island

Parade Ground

See Buda, Important Streets and Squares, Disz tér

Paris Court

See Felszabadulás tér

Parliament Building (Országház)   C/D4(L3)

Location
V, Kossuth Lajos tér

Underground Station
M2 (Kossuth tér)

Trams
2, 2A

Trolleybuses
70, 78

The Parliament Building, which is considered one of the oustanding achievements of modern architecture in the Hungarian capital, was constructed between 1885 and 1902 to plans by Emmerich Steindl. It is situated between Kossuth Lajos tér and the Danube (see entries) and is one of the landmarks of Budapest. The building is 268 m (820 ft) long, up to 118 m (387 ft) wide, and consists of a central range with a dome (96 m (315 ft) high), two 73 m (240 ft) high towers on the loggia facing the Danube, and in addition two side wings; the southern one is the Chamber of the House of Representatives and the northern one the Congress Hall (formerly the Chamber of the Upper House). Each of these chambers is crowned by a roof bearing four turrets. The imposing façade on the bank of the Danube is embellished with eighty-eight statues including Hungarian hereditary princes, military leaders and kings.

Interior

On the east side a flight of steps leads up to the main doorway which is flanked by two stone lions. On the ceiling of the stairwell are frescoes by K. Lotz and in a niche a bust of the architect Steindl by A. Stróbl.

On the first floor is the fine domed Hall (height 27 m (88 ft)); the dome is supported on sixteen pillars with likenesses of leading Hungarian rulers. In the Hunting Room (Vadászterem) can be seen wall-paintings by A. Körösfői-Kriesch. Behind this, in the Gobelin Room (Gobelinterem), is a colossal wall tapestry which depicts an assembly of Magyar princes at the time of their occupation of the country. The Chamber of the House of Representatives and the Congress Hall are beautifully decorated. In the Munkácsy Room, next to the study of the leader of the Presidential Council, can be seen the great painting by M. Munkácsy "Conquest of the Country" (by the Magyars). The Parliamentary Library (Országgyűlési Könyvtár) has a comprehensive stock of legal, governmental and historical literature; it is reached by the south door on the side of the building facing the Danube.

Parliament Street (Országház utca)

See Buda, Important Streets and Squares

Pauline Monastery

See University Church

People's Park

See Népliget

People's Stadium

See Népstadion

*Pest   C4–F6(K3–N6)

Until its union with Buda and Obuda in 1872, Pest was an independent town, but for a long time its development was difficult, as it was overshadowed by the neighbouring royal town. Nevertheless, for a long time Pest has had close links with Buda. The Romans maintained a "castrum contra Aquincum" at Marcius 15 tér, the purpose of which was to protect the Danube crossing. The Hungarian rulers who resided in Buda visited Pest from time to time to attend services in what is now the Inner City Parish Church (see entry). By the 15th c. Pest had become prosperous. At this period the town was surrounded by fortifications which followed the course of the present Inner Ring.

It was in the 19th c. that Pest attained its greatest prosperity as the town of craftsmen, traders and merchants; this is revealed by the numerous fine buildings which are still standing today. At that time the principal focus of population shifted from the Buda to the Pest side of the Danube. As early as 1830 there were far more than 60,000 people in Buda, the majority of them living in the rapidly growing suburbs. The inner city of Pest forms the central business district of the Hungarian capital. Pest is the headquarters of the most important organs of government, Parliament (see entry), ministries, etc., and leading cultural institutions (universities, museums, churches, etc.).

Location
District V

Underground Lines
M1, M2, M3

Trams
2, 2A, 47, 49

Trolleybuses
70, 72, 73, 78, 83

Buses
1, 2, 4, 4A, 5, 7, 7A, 9, 15, 16, 112, 182

Pest Broadway

See Nagymező utca

Pest Danube Bank

See Danube Corso

Pest District Council

See Municipal Council

Pest Redoubt

See Vigadó

Pest Synagogue E5(M4)

Location
VII, Dohány utca 2

Underground Station
M2 (Astoria)

The Pest Synagogue was built in the last century to the plans of the Viennese architect Ludwig Förster. The romanticised Moorish-Byzantine style of this three-aisled temple is very pleasing; F. Feszl was responsible for the fine interior. Trolleybus 74

Jewish Museum

The Jewish Museum (Országos Zsidó Vallási és Történeti Gyűjtemény) is housed in an annexe of the synagogue; it contains interesting documentation and valuable works of art. On Wesselényi utca is a heroes' temple (1931) for the Jewish soldiers who fell in the First World War.
In the synagogue garden can be seen a cemetery with a memorial to the victims of National Socialism.

Pest Theatre

See Váci utca

*Petőfi Museum (Petőfi Irodalmi Múzeum) E5/6(M5)

Location
VI, Károlyi Mihály utca 16

Bus
15

The museum is dedicated to Sándor Petőfi and contains memorabilia and a collection of texts of the leading Hungarian poet and author. There are journals, manuscripts, books, periodicals, etc., a sound archive and works by various notable artists. From time to time exhibitions on particular themes and on the subject of selected Hungarian authors add to the interest.

Károlyi Palace

The Petőfi Museum is housed in the historical Károlyi Palace, a 19th c. building in Classical style. In 1848/49 the Austrian General Julius Haynau, who was to defeat the freedom fighters, resided here. It was here, too, that Count Lajos Batthyány was arrested in 1848. Mihály Károlyi (1875–1955), politician and Hungarian President from 1918 to 1919, was the owner of this palace. A memorial room has been furnished in his honour.

Petőfi Sándor utca D5(M4/5)

Buses
2, 15

Petőfi Sándor utca, formerly called Uri utca (Gentlemen's Walk), one of the fine highways of Pest, joins the two squares Felszabadulás tér and Martinelli tér (see entries). Together with Váci utca (see entry) and the adjoining streets it forms the principal shopping centre of the Hungarian capital. Buildings notable for their architecture are house No. 3 which dates from the 19th c. to the plans of J. Hild and No. 6, the popular József Katona Theatre (Katona József Színház). Close by (Nos. 13–19) is the Budapest Main Post Office and Telegraph Office.

Petőfi tér   D5(L5)

This square, named after the Hungarian lyric poet Sándor Petőfi (see Notable Personalities) is the venue of the patriotic festivities which take place annually on 15 March. There is a well-proportioned bronze Petőfi monument by Adolf Huszár (1882) in the square.
Buses 2, 15

Location
District V

Trams
2, 2A

On the east side of Petőfi tér is the three-aisled Greek church (Orthodox Egyház templom), erected in 1789 and rebuilt in the 19th c. to the plans of Ybl. Inside this large church there are fine works of art by Nikolaus Jankovits, Anton Kochmeister and others.

Greek church

Pharmaceutical Museum "Golden Eagle"

See Buda, Important Streets and Squares, Tárnok utca

Plague Column

See Buda, Important Streets and Squares, Szentháromság tér

Planetarium

See Népliget

Postal Museum

See Népköztársaság útja

Postal Savings Bank

See Szabadság tér

Premonstratensian Convent

See Margaret Island

Prince Eugene Equestrian Statue

See Castle Palace

Puppet Theatre

See Népköztársaság útja

Rác-fürdó (Rac Baths)

See Tabán

Rákóczi út   E/F5(M/N4)

Location
Boundary between Districts
VII and VIII

Underground Stations
M2 (Astoria, Keleti pu)

Buses
7, 7A, 78

This thoroughfare, named after the leader of the independence movement of the beginning of the 18th c. (see Notable Personalities), is a continuation of Kossuth Lajos utca, from the site of the now-vanished medieval Hatvan town gate on the Inner Ring (see entry) to the East Station (see entry).
Rákóczi út, today one of the main shopping streets of Budapest, is flanked by many large stores (Textiljáz, Versen, Csillag, Lottó and Otthon), and important cultural institutions, for example the Academy of Stage and Film Art (Szinművészeti Főiskola) and the associated Odry Theatre (Odry színpad) at Vas utca. In addition there are leading cinemas (Uránia, No. 21; Tisza, No. 70) and well-known restaurants and cafés (Restaurant Emke, Konditorei Hauer, etc.).
Secular buildings notable for their architecture are No. 5 (1867; formerly a hotel; memorial tablet to Prince Rákóczi) and No. 13 which was built in 1837 to plans by J. Hild.

St Rochus Chapel

The Baroque St Rochus Chapel (Rókus-kápolna) was built in 1711 and extended in 1740. Its tower dates from the end of the 18th c.
Near the chapel is the Rochus Hospital (Rókus-kórház) where Ignaz Philipp Semmelweis (see Notable Personalities) worked between 1851 and 1857. His statue was created in Carrara marble by A. Stróbl.

Redoubt

See Vigadó

Reformed Churches

See Inner Ring, Kálvin tér, China Museum

Roman Excavations

See Obuda, Március 15 tér

*Roosevelt tér   D5(L4)

Location
District V

Trams
2, 2A

The double square at the Pest end of the Chain Bridge commemorates the former US President Franklin D. Roosevelt. At the beginning of the last century markets were held here. Also, until the Chain Bridge was built, there was a mooring-

Hungarian Academy of Science in Roosevelt Square

place for Danube freighters. On the northern side of the square stands a memorial to Széchenyi by J. Engel (1880) and on the south side a Deák memorial by the artist A. Huszár (1882).

Buses
2, 4, 16

*Gresham Palace (Gresham-palota)

D5(L4)

One of the masterpieces of Secessionist style in Budapest is the Gresham Palace built in 1907 to plans by Quittner and the Vágó brothers. This traditional former insurance building is now the seat of the Municipal Tourist Office of Budapest (Budapest Tourist).
Between the two world wars the former Café Gresham was a well-known meeting-place for artists.

Location
V, east side of Roosevelt tér

*Hungarian Academy of Science
(Magyar Tudományos Akadémia)

D5(L4)

The north side of Roosevelt tér is dominated by the monumental building of the Hungarian Academy of Science; in Neo-Renaissance style, it was founded on the initiative of Count Istvan Széchenyi (see Notable Personalities) in 1825. The headquarters of this, now the most eminent scientific institution in Hungary, was completed in 1864. Plans were drawn by the Berlin architect Friedrich August Stüler. The façades of the building are embellished with artistic representations. Also of interest is a bronze relief by Holló (1893) which depicts the foundation of the Academy by Count Széchenyi in 1825.

Location
V, north side of Roosevelt tér

111

The Academy, with which there are now associated a number of research institutes, has a scientific library which is well known even outside the frontiers of the country (especially the Oriental Department). In the restored Festival Hall are fine frescoes by K. Lotz.

Akadémia utca

North-east of the Academy stand two notable Classical buildings: at Akadémia utca 1, completed in 1835 (fine façade with Corinthian wall pillars), there once lived the Polish General József Bem and György Klapka, both renowned fighters in the freedom struggle of 1848/49. Near by at Akadémia utca 3 is an imposing building dating from 1836 by the great architect J. Hild.

Eötvös tér   D5(L4)

Location
V, south of Roosevelt tér

Adjoining Roosevelt tér on the south is the small Eötvös tér with a monument of József Eötvös (see Notable Personalities) by A. Huszár. On the south side of the square stand two luxury hotels, Atrium Hyatt and Forum, which were opened comparatively recently.

*Rose Hill (Rózsadomb)   B/C3

Location
II, west of Margaret Bridge

Buses
11, 91, 191

Rose Hill (Rózsadomb; District II) has long been one of the most exclusive residential areas of the Hungarian capital. Elegant villas, large gardens, avenues and footpaths extend to the Cool Valley (Hüvövöly). On the side of the hill facing the Danube a modern trade union convalescent home is visible from a considerable distance.

Turbe of Gül Baba (Gül Baba türbeje)   C3

Location
Mecset utca 14

Trams
4, 6

Bus
84

In the grounds of an old villa can be found the Turbe (mausoleum) of a Muslim Dervish Gül Baba (Turkish=rose father), which was built between 1543 and 1548. Gül Baba died during a festival in the Matthias Church which had been converted into a mosque. The rather plain octagonal domed building is now a museum (memorials of Gül Baba and the Bektasi Order).

Rottenbill Park

See Köbánya

Rudas Bath

See Gellért Hill

St Andrew (St Andreas)

See Szentendre

St Anne's Church

See Víziváros

St Elisabeth's Church

See Víziváros

St Joseph's Church

See Joseph Town Parish Church

St Nicholas' Tower

See Buda, Important Streets and Squares, Hess András tér

St Rochus Chapel

See Rákóczi ut

*St Stephen's Basilica (Szent István-bazilika)   D5(M4)

St Stephen's Basilica, in Neo-Renaissance style, is one of the most imposing ecclesiastical buildings of the Hungarian capital. The church is of monumental proportions with a central dome, 96 m (315 ft) high, and two 80 m (262 ft) high towers at the west end. Building began in 1851. The plans were largely the work of Josef Hild, the great exponent of Classical architecture. After Hild's death and the collapse of the dome in 1868, Nikolaus Ybl proposed new plans which finally gave the church its great size and Neo-Renaissance style. After Ybl's death Josef Kauser completed St Stephen's Church, which is at present being restored at considerable cost.

Magnificent works of art adorn the interior: by the first pillar on the right supporting the dome can be seen a group of figures by A. Stróbl which portray Bishop Gellért and St Emmerich. On the second pillar on the right is King Ladislaus the Holy, a work of János Fadrusz; on the second pillar on the left there is a statue of St Elisabeth by K. Senyci. The mosaics on the dome were produced in the Salviati workshop in Venice to sketches by Karl Lotz. At the magnificent High Altar is a statue of St Stephen made of Carrara marble by A. Stróbl. On the wall of the apse the bronze reliefs by E. Mayer depict scenes from the life of St Stephen, and the pictures in the side altars are also very fine. Of particular note is the painting on the second altar to the right of the main entrance. It is a work by Gyula Benczúr and shows St Stephen offering the Hungarian crown to Mary.

Location
V, Szent István tér

Underground Station
M1 (Bajcsy Zsilinszky út)

Buses
4, 4A, 6, 16

Interior

St Stephen's Basilica

State Opera House, interior

Fessler Statues

The Fessler statues are one of the special features of St Stephen's Basilica. On the exterior wall of the apse the Twelve Apostles can be seen; the Four Evangelists stand in niches on the outside of the dome; in niches on the towers of the main façade are likenesses of the Fathers of the Church and in the tympanum of the narthex the Patrona Hungariae, surrounded by Hungarian saints.

Semmelweis Museum

See Tabán

Semmelweis University

See Üllői út

Serbian Church

See Váci utca

Silk Spinning Mill

See Obuda

South Station (Déli pályaudvar)   **B5(L7)**

The very modern South Station was completed in 1977 to plans by the architect G. Kővári. It is the terminus for trains from Lake Balaton (see entry) and from southern Transdanubia. In the semi-circular station forecourt – terminus of underground (Metro) line 2 – is a work in enamel by Viktor Vasarély. Underground Station M2 (Déli pu.). Trams 18, 59, 61. Buses 5, 12, 21, 39.

Location
1, Alkotás utca-Krisztina körút

On the north side of the station lies an open space which in 1795 became known as the "Meadow of Blood" (Vermező), where the instigators of the Hungarian Jacobin movement were executed. On the north side of the present park a monument commemorates this event. After the Second World War the area was raised about 2 m (6 ft) with debris and laid out as a park, in the centre of which is an anti-Fascist memorial by I. Szabó (1967).

Meadow of Blood

In Krisztina tér, south-east of the South Station stands the Christinatown Parish Church (Krisztina-városi plébánia-templom) which was built in the 18th c.

Christinatown Parish Church

Spa Establishments

See Practical Information

Square of 15 March

See Marcius 15 tér

Stadium

See Népstadion

*State Opera (Allami Operaház)   **D/E4(M3)**

Nikolaus Ybl drew up the plans for the prestigious State Opera, which was built between 1875 and 1884 in Neo-Renaissance style.
Arcades, which bear a balcony with balustrades, protect the carriage entrance. In the two niches on either side are statues of Franz Liszt and Ferenc Erkels, the first Director of the opera, by A. Stróbl.
On the first storey of the main façade is a loggia; in each of the two corner pillars two allegorical figures have been let in. On the balustrade of the first storey are statues of famous composers by the Hungarian artists G. Donáth, G. Kiss and A. Stróbl.

Location
VI, Népköztársaság útja 22

Underground Station
M1 (Opera)

Buses
1, 4, 4A

Interior	The interior of the State Opera boasts a magnificent foyer with a double marble staircase. B. Székely created the ceiling-frescoes; the wall-paintings portraying scenes from Greek mythology are the work of Mór Than. A. Stróbl fashioned the bust of Ybl.
	The auditorium boasts unusually good acoustics. The Royal Box, which has been restored to its original form, and the retiring-room are redolent of the elegance of yester-year. The ceiling-frescoes by K. Lotz and the wall-paintings by Mór Than are masterpieces of their kind.
State Ballet Institute	Opposite the Opera is the State Ballet Institute (Allami Ballett-intézet), which was created in 1883 to plans by the architects Lechner and Pártos.

Street of the People's Republic

See Népköztársaság útja

Szabadság hid

See Freedom Bridge

*Szabadság tér (Freedom Square)   D4(L3)

Location District V	Freedom Square, laid out in the last century after a barracks where many Hungarian freedom fighters of 1848/49 were executed was pulled down, forms with the surrounding buildings one of the most charming architectural ensembles of Budapest. On its west side stands the former Exchange, now the headquarters of Hungarian Television; on the east side is the Hungarian National Bank (Magyar Nemzeti Bank). Both these functional buildings were the work of the architect Ignác Alpár and date from 1905. The former Exchange is in Secessionist style, while the National Bank is a first-class example of a Late Classical building.
Underground Station M2 (Kossuth tér)	
Bus 15	
National Bank	
	In the centre of the semicircular northern end of the square stands a Soviet memorial (obelisk) with a relief by the artist Károly Antal (1945). The northern arc is lined by buildings in the Neo-Romanesque-Eclectic manner.
Former Postal Savings Bank	Near the bank, but oriented towards Rosenberg házaspár utca, is the former Postal Savings Bank (No. 4) by Edmund Lechner, who was here anxious to create a new Hungarian architectural style. The building, which was opened in 1901, is characterised by variegated majolica decoration from the porcelain factory at Pécs.

Széchenyi-lanchid

See Chain Bridge

Széchenyi National Library

See Castle Palace

Széna tér (Hay Square)

See Moszkva tér

---

*Szentendre (St Andrew)

The romantic little town of Szentendre (101 m (331 ft); pop. 16,000) is situated on the hilly right bank of the Danube to the north of Budapest. In the past many artists were attracted within its boundaries. Meanwhile tourists have also "discovered" the town.

The origins of the settlement go back to the 4th c. BC when the Celts were here. About the time of Christ's birth the Romans set up a military camp. The first mention of the place is in 1146 and from the 14th c. several waves of Serbs arrived. In the 18th c. Szentendre experienced an economic upsurge (trade centre) and became a Pravo-Slav bishopric.

The chief square in Szentendre is the triangular Marx tér, in which stands an 18th c. merchants' cross, a masterpiece of wrought-iron work.

On the Danube side of this square is the Greek Orthodox Blagoveštenska Church which was built in the middle of the 18th c. to plans by Andreas Mayerhoffer. It contains an iconostasis in Rococo style. On the north adjoining the church is the Ferenczy Károly Múzeum (Marx tér 6), with works by the artist family of Ferenczy (paintings, sculptures, tapestries) and

Location
20 km (12 miles) north of Budapest

Access
HEV line
Budapest-Szentendre.
In summer boats from Budapest (Vigadó tér)

Sights
Marx tér

Blagoveštensak Church

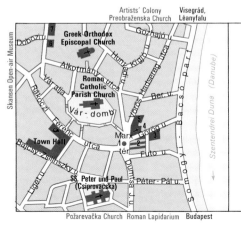

Szentendre
Town Centre

1 Merchant's Cross
2 Picture Gallery
3 Blagoveštenska Church
4 Margit-Kovács Collection
5 Ferenczy Museum
6 Museum of Serbian Ecclesiastical Art
7 Cultural Centre

100 m
110 yd

Szentendre

Szentendre, inner town

Detail in the Skanzen open-air Museum

numerous exhibits of local history (archaeological finds, Hungarian and Serbian costumes, etc.).

Margit-Kovács Collection

On the south side of the Blagoveštenska Church can be found the collection of the ceramic artist Margit Kovács (d. 1977) who combined traditional popular art and modern elements in her work.

Roman Catholic Parish Church

Above Marx tér on Várdomb Castle Hill (fine views) stands the Roman Catholic church, the origins of which go back to a 13th c. building. Parts of the present, predominately 18th c., church are of 14th and 15th c. dates. The interior contains modern frescoes. Opposite the church the works of the painter Béla Czóbel (1883–1976) are presented in a fitting setting.

Greek Orthodox Episcopal Church

The Greek Orthodox Episcopal church, which was completed in 1764 is situated in the upper part of Alkótmány utca. Its Rococo doorway and the fine carving of the iconastasis are worthy of note. In the courtyard a collection of Serbian Church art (Szerb Egyházművészeti Gyűjtemény) can be seen.

Cultural Centre

Nearby on the north in Engels utca is the Cultural Centre (Művelődési Központ és Könyvtár), with a fine mosaic by Jenő Barcsay.

Town Hall

To the south of Castle Hill is the Baroque Town Hall (Városi Tanács) and the 18th c. Catholic Church of Peter and Paul (Péter-Pál-templom) which is the successor to a Pravo-Slav Ciprovačka Church.

Along the road from the town centre southwards to the HEV Station is the Baroque Požarevačka Church, dedicated in 1763; this is a Greek Orthodox church with a wonderful icon wall in Byzantine style. To the south-west of this church in Római Sánc utca are the remains of a former Roman camp.

Požarevačka Church

To the north of Marx tér in Vörös Hadsereg útja stands the Greek Orthodox Preobraženska Church, built in 1740, which is one of the finest Pravo-Slav churches in Szentendre. Further to the north is an artists' colony which came into being in 1928 and where today more than three dozen artists are busy. Periodic exhibitions can be seen in an adjoining gallery.

Preobraženska Church

Artists' Colony

About 3 km (2 miles) north of the town centre is the folklore museum of Skanzen which is still being developed, where rural buildings, houses, mills, churches and other architectural features from various regions of Hungary have been re-erected in their original style. Inside some of the buildings can be seen traditional furnishings and articles of everyday use and this enables the visitor to gain a comprehensive idea of life in provincial Hungary.

*Open-air Museum
Skanzen

A few kilometres north of Szentendre lies the first-class holiday resort of Léányfalu (a boating harbour on the Danube, camping site, bathing beaches, etc.) which was popular with artists and men of letters as early as the beginning of the 19th c.

Léányfalu

Szentháromság tér

See Buda, Important Streets and Squares

Szentháromság utca

See Buda, Important Streets and Squares

Szent István körút

See Outer Ring

*Tabán

C5/6(M/N8)

The district of Tabán lies in the depression between Castle Hill and Gellért Hil (see entry). During the time of the Turkish occupation Tamils particularly were settled here. In the 18th c. there was an influx of Serbian refugees whose simple dwellings were not removed until the 1930s.
Extensive parks and traffic layouts are features of the modern district.

Location
District I

Trams
8, 8A, 9, 18, 19, 112

Buses
5, 78, 86

*Semmelweis Museum (Semmelweis Orvostörténeti Múzeum)   C5(N8)

At the foot of Castle Hill on the south-east side stands the 18th c. house (renovated in the 19th c.) in which the famous Hungarian

Location
1, Apród utca 1–3

doctor, Ignaz Philipp Semmelweis (see Notable Personalities) was born. It is now furnished as a museum of the history of medicine and includes documents and objects left by Ignaz Philipp Semmelweis, medical implements and instruments and pharmaceutical utensils.

*Golden Stag (Arany Szarvas)   C5(N8)

Location
1, Szarvas tér 1

This famous old inn is furnished in the ''pigtail'' style of the 19th c. From this triangular building steps lead up to the castle which still has some pretty architectural details of the last century.

*Tabán Parish Church (Tabáni plébánia-templom)   C5(N8)

Location
1, Szarvas tér

This Baroque church with only a single tower is dedicated to St Catherine of Alexandria. It was built between 1728 and 1740 and replaced a medieval church which existed at that time and which, during the Turkish occupation, was a mosque known as Mustafa Camii.

One of the treasures of the Tabán Parish Church is a carved figure (called the ''Tabán Christ'') below the gallery. It is a copy of a figure dating from the 12th c. and the original can be seen in the Castle Museum. In a niche is a representation of St Florian, no doubt inspired by the disastrous conflagration of Tabán in 1810. The frescoes were the work of Kimnach (1890).

Ybl Miklós tér (Nicholas Ybl Square)   C5(N8)

Location
1, Danube Bank

Below the castle on the bank of the Danube lies the square named after the famous architect Nicholas (Miklós) Ybl (1814–91). His monument in the centre of the square was the work of E. Mayer (1896). Round the square stand buildings designed by Ybl and he was also responsible for the splendid flight of steps (1882), with arcades and niches, which leads up to the castle.

The 310 m (340 yd) long castle bazaar (Várbazár) always attracts many tourists to its shops, artists' studios and inns. In the warm months of the year dancing and entertainment take place on its terrace.

Rác-fürdó (Emmerich Baths, Imre-fürdó)   C5(N8)

Location
1, Hadnagy utca

The Rac Baths which are situated to the south of Tabán Parish Church were established and extended in the Turkish period. The medicinal springs were known as early as the 15th c.

Tanács körút

See Inner Ring

Táncsics Mihály utca

See Buda, Important Streets and Squares

Tárnok utca

See Buda, Important Streets and Squares

Terézváros (Theresa's Town)   D–F4/5(M/N3/4)

This former suburb of Pest has managed to retain its character of the first half of the 19th c.

Along Majakovszkij utca can be seen an exemplary range of Classical dwellings. Of especial merit is the former house of a goldsmith (No. 11), dating from 1810 with an articulated façade. Farther on is a building (No. 47) designed by A. Pollack in 1848, which is in the Romantic style.

Location
District V

Underground Station
M2 (Opera, Hősök tere)

Theresa Town Parish Church   E4/5(N3)
(Terézvárosi plébánia-templom)

This church was built to designs by F. Kasselik at the beginning of the 19th c. Originally it was in "pigtail" style but a few decades later it was rebuilt in Neo-Baroque. The High Altar by M. Pollack is of special merit. The beautiful chandelier formerly hung in the Pest Redoubt (see Vigadó).

Location
Corner of Majakovszkij/
Nagymező utca

Trolleybuses
70, 78

Theatre of Comedy

See Outer Ring, Szent István körút

Thermal Spa Hotel

See Margaret Island

Tolbuhin tér

See Inner Ring

Transport Museum

See City Woodland Park

Trinity Square

See Buda, Important Streets and Squares

Trinity Street

See Buda, Important Streets and Squares

Ujlak Parish Church (Ujlaki plébánia-templom)   C2

Location
II, corner Bécsi út/Szép-völgyi út

Tram
17

The Baroque Parish Church of Ujlak, a settlement which was in existence in the Middle Ages as an independent community, was built in the 18th c. to plans by Chr. Hamom and M. Nepauer. On the High Altar which is the work of Hickisch can be seen a picture by Falconer and a copy of a "Madonna" by Lukas Cranach.

Üllői út   E6–J8(N5/6)

Location
Boundary between Districts VIII, IX and X

Underground Stations
M3 (Kálvin tér, Népliget)

Bus
182

Üllői út leads from Kálvin tér (see entry) along an arterial road to the south-east. The section near the centre is flanked by a number of very well-maintained Classical buildings. Of especial note are No. 7, No. 17 which was the work of M. Pollack and M. Ybl and once the residence of the composer Ferenc Erkel, and some older buildings of the Budapest Clinic. South-east of the Museum of Applied Arts (see entry) with its notable architecture, are buildings of the turn of the century as well as other departments of the clinic.

Kun Béla tér

Kun Béla tér, which is hemmed in between buildings of the clinic and the Botanical Garden of the University (see entry) has a particular charm because of the monument unveiled in 1967 commemorating three of the prominent leaders of the Hungarian-Societ Republic (Béla Kun, Jeno Landler and Tibor Szamuely); the monument was a combined work by the artists A. Farkas, K. Herczeg and Z. O. Kiss.

Semmelweis University

On Nagyvárad tér farther south-east, a twenty-three-storey building is one of the tallest landmarks of the Hungarian capital. In it a number of important departments of the Semmelweis University of Medicine are housed.
Opposite to the south is the clinic of the district of Ferencváros with the Cardiological Institute. There are a number of sports grounds in the vicinity.

Underground Railway Museum

See Inner Ring, Deák Ferenc tér

Union Monument

See Margaret Island

Universities

Karl Marx University   See Dimitrov tér

Loránd-Eötvös University   See entry

Semmelweis University   See Ullői út

*University Church (Egyetemi templom)   D/E6 (M5)

The University Church, probably the most beautiful Baroque church in Budapest, was built between 1725 and 1742 to plans by Andreas Mayerhoffer for the Pauline Order established in Hungary. Its two mighty towers were completed in 1770/71. The principal façade includes a triangular gable with a representation of the hermits Paul and Anthony as well as the arms of the Pauline Order (a palm between two lions and a raven).

Location
V, Eötvös Loránd utca 5–7

Bus
15

The University Church has a nave and a side chapel. The frescoes on the ceiling (scenes from the life of Mary) are the work of a J. Bergl (1776). The choir-stalls and the sculptures of the nativity of Mary together with St Paul and St Antony were carved by Josef Hebenstreit (1746). The copy of the "Black Madonna from Tschenstochau" was probably completed about 1720.
Pauline monks of various workshops were responsible for the pulpit, the pews, the doors and the sacristy cupboards which are decorated with intarsia work. The cupboards contain valuable monstrances, chalices and ecclesiastical vestments.

Interior

The former Pauline Monastery near the church (18th c.; architect: Matthias Drenker) has housed since 1805 the Theological Faculty of the first Hungarian University which was transferred in 1784 to Pest.
The library, finished in 1775, has richly decorated bookcases, a gallery running round it and a spiral staircase with pierced balustrades and banisters. The ceiling-fresco was created by Pietro Rivetti in 1803.

Pauline Monastery

Úri utca

See Buda, Important Streets and Squares.

*Vác

The town of Vác (111 m (364 ft); pop. 34,000) lies on the strip of land between the northern Hungarian Uplands and the Alföld. It was already a bishopric in the 11th c. It suffered greatly during the Turkish occupation and lost almost all its medieval buildings. In 1846 the first railway in Hungary was opened between Vác and Budapest. Today Vác is a thriving industrial town (building materials, chemicals, shipbuilding).

Location
34 km (21 miles) north of Budapest

Access
By rail from Budapest, Nyugati pu.

The main square of Vác is Konstantin tér, laid out in the Baroque style. Here the Cathedral stands, (1763–77) built to plans of I. Canevale; its beautiful frescoes in the dome and the murals in the choir are the work of the artist Maulbertsch. In the Cathedral Treasury notable goldsmiths' work of the Renaissance and the Baroque periods can be seen. Opposite the cathedral is the Bishop's Palace of 1775 and to the south the Vak-Bottyán

Sights

Cathedral

Vak-Bottyán Museum

Váci utca

Váci utca

Vigadó, interior

Museum (Múzeum utca 4) which contains exhibits concerning the history of the town.

Trinity Square

Not far north of the Cathedral lies Trinity Square with a beautiful Trinity Column dedicated in 1755. On the east side of the square is a Baroque church (18th c.), the origins of which go back to a church of the Piarists.

Square of 15 March

The Square of 15 March, formerly the town market-place, is surrounded by fine Baroque buildings. The imposing Parish Church of the Upper Town (Felsővárosi plébánia-templom; 18th c.) has Rococo elements. Close by stands the 18th c. Town Hall (Városi Tanácsház; 18th c.) and the Deaf and Dumb Institute, dating from 1802.

Triumphal Gate

In the north of the Inner Town in Köztársaság útja rises a Triumphal Gate designed by I. Canevale in 1764 commemorating the Empress Maria Theresa.

Surroundings

Some 11 km (7 miles) south-east of Vác near Vácrátót is the arboretum of the Hungarian Academy of Science, in a park extending over 24 ha (59 acres), laid out in the last century. In the park several thousand species of trees can be studied.

---

*Váci utca

D5/6(L/M4/5)

Váci utca leads from Vörösmarty tér (see entry) first to Felszabadulás tér (see entry) and on to Dimitrov tér (see entry).

Its northern sector is the leading shopping street of the Hungarian capital and quite recently was made a pedestrian zone. Here there is a succession of stores, boutiques, footwear and leather shops, bookshops, jewellers, arts and crafts shops, expressos, and last but not least, the offices of the leading airline companies.

Location
District V

Underground Stations
M1, M2, M3 (Deák tér) M3
(Felszabadulás tér)

The Pest theatre (Pesti Színház; No. 9) occupies the former "Hotel of the Seven Electoral Princes", where the eleven-year-old Franz Liszt gave his first concert in Pest in 1823. The foyer of the theatre with its beautiful dark mosaic work is very impressive.

Pest Theatre

The new Town Hall (Uj Városház; Nos. 62–64) was built by the architect E. Steindl in Neo-Renaissance style between 1869 and 1875. There are wonderful mosaics by K. Lotz in the Council Chamber.

New Town Hall

The Serbian church (Szerb templom; No. 66) was probably designed by the famous architect Andreas Mayerhoffer in the 18th c. Especially impressive is its façade with a single high tower. The nave has three articulated parts. The women's section on a higher level is separated from the men's section by a wooden balustrade. Higher still lies the Solea with the seat of the prelate. The iconostasis, which divides the choir from the nave, was painted in the middle of the 19th c. by K. Sterio and is characterised by features showing the influence of Italian Renaissance paintings.

Serbian Church

Vajdahunyad

See City Woodland Park

Városliget

See City Woodland Park

Városmajor (Municipal Farm, Park)   A/B4

Városmajor Park, about 10 ha (25 acres) in extent has tennis-courts, games areas and footpaths, and on fine days attracts very many citizens of Budapest seeking relaxation. The old trees, which were planted here more than a century ago, are a particularly charming feature.

Location
XII, Szilágyi Erzsébet Fasor-
Városmajor utca

Buses
5, 18, 22, 28, 56, 56E, 156,
158

On the north side of the park is the Hotel Budapest, an imposing circular tower block (18 storeys, 560 beds) designed by G. Szrogh.

Hotel Budapest

A cog-wheel railway (Fogaskerekű vasút) in the western part of the park ascends to Széchenyi-hegy from which there are panoramic views.

Cog-wheel Railway

Vigadó, façade overlooking the Danube

Open-air Theatre

In the eastern part of Városmajor Park is an open-air theatre with more than 1000 seats for spectators, as well as a Catholic church, designed by A. and B. Arkay, which has frescoes by V. Aba-Novák and stained-glass windows by L. Arkay.

On Városmajor utca, south of the park, can be seen houses built in Romantic and Classical styles.

Várpalota

See Castle Palace

Vidám Park

See City Woodland Park, Amusement park

Villa of Hercules

See Obuda

Vienna Gate Square

See Buda, Important Streets, and Squares, Bécsi kapu tér

*Vigadó (Pest Redoubt)   D5(L4)

The Vigadó built 1859 to plans by Frigyes Feszl, is among the most remarkable examples of Hungarian Romantic architecture. Intended for festival occasions and all kinds of musical entertainment, the Vigadó was severely damaged at the end of the Second World War, but after very many years of restoration it was again opened in 1980.

The side of the Pest Redoubt facing the Danube is exceptionally noteworthy: each of the two projecting sections on the flanks is borne on two pillars topped with crowns, with representations of King Béla IV and Judge Jakob Valuta, in addition to figures of dancers. On the upper floor of the centre range, between the tall arched windows, can be seen allegorical figures. Above the window arches are a frieze with the Hungarian coat of arms, figures of the two kings Louis I and Matthias Corvinus by János Hunyadi and Miklós Zrinyi, as well as statues of the Palatine Jószef and Count Széchenyi.

On the square in front of the Vigadó stands the Soviet monument and on the south side of Vigadó tér the luxury hotel, Duna Intercontinental.

Location
V, Vigadó tér

Underground Station
M1 (Vörösmarty tér)

Trams
2, 2A

Buses
2, 15

Boat Landing Stage
Vigadó

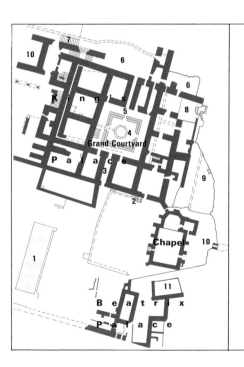

Visegrád
Royal Palace
Királyi palota

1 Foundation of Grand Staircase

2 New Staircase

3 Corridor

4 Hercules Fountain (red marble)

5 Gothic Cloister

6 North Rock Court

7 North Steps

8 Bath

9 Lion Fountain

10 Cellar

11 Great Hall in Beatrix Palace

**Visegrád

Location
42 km/30 miles north of
Budapest

Access
Bus and boat from Budapest

Visegrád (108 m (354 ft), pop. 2500) has an exceptionally picturesque situation on the loop of the Danube in the Hungarian Wachau and is one of the most-visited tourist venues in Hungary.

The Romans maintained a fortification at this strategically favourable place; there is a reconstruction of a watch-tower near Fó utca. In the 9th c. AD the Slavs settled here (Slav "Višegrad" = elevated fortress). Later the Magyars pressed forward and occupied the fortress. Right up to the 14th c. the Hungarian Royal Crown was kept in the stronghold.

Sights
King's Palace
(Királyi palota)

Above Fó utca in the north of Visegrád are the remains of a King's Palace which was begun in the first half of the 14th c. and which, with its sumptuous buildings and courtyards, once covered an area of 600 m (660 yds) × 300 m (330 yds). The palace was extended by Kings Charles Robert of Anjou, Sigismund of Luxemburg and Matthias I. Corvinus and was finally completed by Italian builders. Altogether it is said to have had 350 rooms and to have been very richly furnished. At the end of the 17th c. the palace was unoccupied and gradually decayed. In 1934 the architect Schulek strove to preserve what was left of the Gothic and Renaissance building of the former royal residence.

Solomon's Tower
(Salomon-torony)

Solomon's Tower (originally 30 m (98 ft) high) was erected in the 13th c. and is a mighty relic of the lower castle of Visegrád; the walls are up to 8 m (26 ft) thick! From this hexagonal tower a wall extends to the bastion on the bank of the Danube. The name of the tower probably comes from a previous building in which King Solomon is said to have been kept prisoner in the 11th c.

King Matthias Museum

Solomon's Tower is now used as the King Matthias Museum. It contains very well-preserved artefacts from the ruined King's Palace, for example, floor tiles and part of a Hercules Fountain.

Stronghold/Citadel
(Fellygvár)

High above the Danube at an elevation of 315m (1,034 ft; footpath and panoramic road) on a site from which there are splendid views, stand the mighty ruins of the Visegrád Stronghold, built on a triangular plan. Building began in 1241 after the attack by the Tartars, that is in the time of King Béla IV. The heart of the fortress is surrounded by several rings of walls and protected by a system of gates, narrow passages and drawbridges. The best-preserved part of the ruins is the East Gatetower which is one of the most interesting examples of Hungarian fortress architecture.

Churches and Chapels

The Catholic parish church in Fó tér is a fine example of Baroque architecture. Higher up on a rock stands a Calvary Chapel of 1770. The Chapel of St Mary on the bank of the Danube was built by followers of Duke Charles of Lorraine in the 18th c.

Surroundings of Visegrád

From Nagyvillám (378 m (1240 ft; hotel) not far from the castle one can look over broad areas of the Pilis range and the Börzsöny Mountains.
There is a footpath from Visegrád to the Pilis Park Forest (Pilisi

Wall fountain in the Royal Palace of Visegrád

Parkerdő) with a nature reserve and the wildly romantic
Lepence Valley.
Some 6 km (4 miles) from Visegrád lies the village of Dormos
near the remains of the well-known Protestant church.

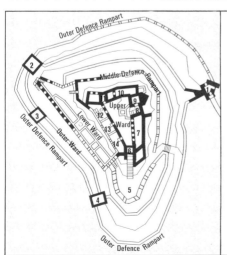

Visegrád
Citadel/Fellegvár

1 East Gate Tower
2 North-west Gate Tower
3 West Gate Tower
4 South-west Gate Tower
5 South Bastion
6 Inner Gate Tower
7 East Palace Range, Chapel
8 Queen's Treasury
9 Treasury Tower
10 Provision Store
11 North Palace Range
12 Matthias Steps
13 Knights' Hall
14 South-west Palace Range

View from Castle Hill of Viziváros, Danube and Parliament Building

*Viziváros   C3–5(M6/7)

Viziváros, the "Water Town" occupies a narrow terrace between Castle Hill and the Danube. Right up until the Turkish period it was fortified. The Turks set up baths in the part of the town which was chiefly inhabited by fishermen, handworkers and merchants and they turned the existing churches into mosques.

A great deal of building went on in the Baroque Age and this is when, among others, St Anne's Church arose. Since the end of the last century the townscape has altered considerably by the building of several storeyed blocks of flats.

The widening of the Danube led to the sinking of the water-table and as a consequence some of the older buildings subsided and these could only be preserved by means of expensive technology.

Location
District I

HEV Station
Batthyány tér

Underground Station
M2 (Batthyány tér)

Trams
9. 19

Buses
11, 39, 42, 60, 86

* St Anne's Church (Szent Anna-templom)   C4(M6)

St Anne's Church, which was built between 1740 and 1758, to plans by Christoph Hamom and Matthäus Nepauer on a rectangular plan, is one of the most beautiful Baroque buildings in present-day Hungary. It was painstakingly restored in the 19th c. and again after the Second World War.

The main façade with its two perfectly formed towers is very beautiful. It is decorated with statues by Leonhard Eber and

Location
I, south side of Batthyány tér

◀ *St Anne's Church in the "Water Town"*

131

Anton Eberhard. In the centre are St Anne and the Virgin Mary. The civic arms of Buda and a symbol of the Trinity can be seen on the tympanum.

P. C. Molnár and B. Kontuly painted the frescoes on the oval cupola of the nave in 1938. The fresco in the choir, representing the Trinity, was done by G. Vogl in 1772. The High Altar, surrounded by pillars and magnificent in its Baroque decoration (St Anne with her daughter Mary in the Temple of Jerusalem) is by K. Bebó who also designed the pulpit.

In the side altars are fine sculptures by Anton Eberhard and splendid paintings by the Viennese artist Franz Wagenschön.

*Batthyány tér   C4(M6)

HEV stop
Batthyány tér

Underground Station
M2 (Batthyány tér)

Trams
9, 19

Buses
11, 39, 42, 60, 86

This square is named after Count Lajos Batthyány (see Notable Personalities) and has always been the centre of Viziváros. Formerly a market was held here and it is now the terminus of the suburban railway HEV from Szentendre to Budapest and of several bus routes and has an Underground station.

Apart from St Anne's Church there are other notable buildings round the square. The former White Cross Inn (No. 4) was adapted by joining two buildings in 1770. While the right-hand wing reveals Baroque tendencies, the left is Rococo. Behind the arched doorway between the two courtyards a transverse wing was built in the 19th c. Here even theatrical performances and dances could be held. The wrought-iron balustrades on the balconies are also very fine. No. 3, the Hickisch House (Hickisch-ház), was built in 1795 in the "pigtail" style. The Four Seasons are represented on the reliefs. On the north side of the square stands the former Franciscan monastery (19th c.); in front of it stands a memorial by Ede Kallos honouring the poet who wrote the Hungarian National Anthem.

St Elisabeth's Church (Szent Erzsébet-templom)   C4(M6/7)

Location
I, Fó utca 41–43

This Baroque church, erected in 1757 on the foundations of a Turkish building, originally belonged to the Franciscans. In 1785 it was transferred to the Order of Elisabeth which maintained a hospital here, now an old people's home. The statues on the façade of the church and the pulpit fashioned by Franciscan monks are well worth seeing.

*The König Baths (Király-fürdo)   C4

Location
I, Fó utca 82–86

The König Baths have nothing to do with kings. They were the property in the last century of a family named König and are among the most interesting establishments of their kind in Budapest. The oldest part of the buildings, which were severely damaged in the Second World War, is the very well-renovated Hamam (Turkish=bath) built in 1570 under Mustafa Pasa. Its eight-sided main room has a gently curved cupola above it and smaller cupolas ornament the three subsidiary rooms. In the Baroque period the baths were considerably extended and received a beautiful vaulted corridor. In 1827 a Classical wing and a pillared courtyard were added.

St Florian's Chapel (Szent Flórián-kápolna)   C4

This little church is by the architect Matthäus Nepauer (1759/ 60). It is at present used as a local church by adherents of the Greek Catholic faith. On the façade of St Florian's are fine statues of St Nicholas, St Florian and St Blaise. There were once pictures and sculptures by F. Wagenschön, J. Weber and others inside the church but these are now in the Historical Museum on Castle Hill (see entry).
Opposite St Florian's Chapel stands the Hungarian Foreign Ministry (Külügyminisztérium).

Location
I, Fő utca 88

Bem József tér   C4

In this square is a monument by J. Istók (1934) commemorating József Bem, a Polish officer who ranged himself in 1848 on the side of the Hungarian freedom fighters. On the plinth of the memorial can be seen works by the lyric poet Sándor Petofi (see Notable Personalities) who was Bem's Adjutant.

Former Café Friedl   C5(M7)

This building, the origins of which go back to the 15th c, was rebuilt in the 18th c. and in 1811 received its neat "pigtail" façade. The corner oriel, crowned by a tower, and the reliefs beneath the windows are very pretty.
The Biedermeier furnishing dates from the middle of the 19th c.

Location
Fő, utca 20

Corvin tér   C4/5(M7)

Around Corvin Square, with a fountain by B. Holló (1904), are a number of notable 18th c. building (Nos. 2, 3, 4, and 5). On the south side of the square is the former Capuchin monastery with a church which still shows considerable Turkish influence in its architecture and ornamentation. On the north side stands the former Buda Redoubt, now the headquarters of the Institute of Popular Education and the home of the national art group which has now become quite celebrated.

*Foundry Museum (Öntödei Múzeum)   C4

The iron-foundry, built in the middle fo the last century by Abraham Ganz, is the core of the industrial complex Ganz (locomotives, wagons, cranes, etc.) which has since become well known far beyond the boundaries of Hungary. The old foundry has quite recently been established as a museum of industrial history.

Location
Bem József u. 20

Bus
11

---

*Vörösmarty tér   D5 (L4)

This square, commemorating the writer Mihály Vörösmarty (see Notable Personalities), lies in the centre of Pest city. The marble monument to the poet was the work of the artists Kallós

Location
District V

Vörösmarty Monument in Vörösmarty Square

Underground Station M1 (Vörösmarty tér)	and Telcs (1908). On the plinth of the memorial twenty-four people are represented, who are reciting Vörösmarty's "Szózat". Round the square are faithfully restored commercial offices. On the west side of the square can be seen the rear of the Cultural Centre (see Vigadó).
Café Gerbeaud	On the north side of Vörösmarty tér can be found the renowned Café Gerbeaud (sometimes known as Café Vörösmarty), which was a popular meeting-place as early as the beginning of this century. A tasteful 19th c. interior and magnificent pastries now attract large numbers of tourists. This café, which has been famous for a long time, was founded in 1858 by H. Kugler and taken over in 1884 by the Swiss E. Gerbeaud. Under his direction the café and pâtisserie has become well known far beyond the borders of the Hungarian capital.

West Station

See Outer Ring, Marx tér

Ybl Miklós tér

See Tabán

Zichy Castle

See Obuda

Zoological–Botanical Garden

See City Woodland Park

Zsigmond tér   C3

Zsigmond tér is the most important road junction in the north
of Buda. The Trinity Column, set up here in 1733 and which
was designed by Ceresola, is worthy of note. The figures on it
are by the artists Barbier, Ferretti and Vogl.

Tram
17

Buses
6, 60, 60A, 86, 111

Practical Information

Airlines (selection)

Budapest	British Airways, V, Apáczai Cs. J. u. 5, tel. 183–299 Pan American, V, Apáczai Cs. J. u. 4, tel. 171–441 Malév, V, Dorottya u. 2, tel: 184–333, Airport: 572–122
New York	British Airways, 530 Fifth Ave., tel. 1–800–AIRWAYS Pan American, 600 Fifth Ave., tel. 800–221–1111 Malév, 630 Fifth Ave., tel. 212–727–6446

Airport (repülőtér)

Ferihegy	Ferihegy International Airport is situated 14 km (9 miles) south-east from the city centre and links the Hungarian capital with the most important European and overseas centres.
Information	Information service at the airport, tel: 572–122.
Airport bus	Express bus connection between Ferihegy Airport and Pester Engels tér is provided by Volán, the National Bus Company, tel. 182-122 or 172-562. By bus (service 93) from the Underground station Kőbánya-Kispest (Metro line 3) to the airport (and vice versa).

Antiques

BAV	The Bizományi Aruház (BAV) agency advises customers who propose to purchase antiques. The headquarters of BAV is situated in Budapest IX, Kinizsi u. 12, tel: 176–511. Works of art, pictures, carpets and furniture are on sale in various specialist shops. The BAV advises customers about Customs and export regulations.

Art Exhibitions and Galleries

Selection	Art Gallery, I, Táncsics Mihály u. 5 Castle Theatre Gallery (Várszínház), I, Szinház u. 1–3 Gallery of the Municipal Council (Főv. Tanács Galériája), V, Szabadsajtó út 5 Helikon Gallery, V, Eötvös Loránd u. 8 István-Csók Gallery, V, Váci u. 25 Art Gallery (Műcsarnok, XIV, Hősök tere Vigadó Gallery (Vigadó), V, Vigadó tér 2

Banks

Opening times	The branches of the Hungarian National Bank (MNB) and the State Savings Bank (OTP) are open Mon–Thurs 8 a.m.–5 p.m., Fri. 8 a.m.–2 p.m.

Branches of the National Bank and Savings Bank as well as authorised bureaux de change exchange money, travellers' cheques and Eurocheques.

Changing money

Baths

See Spas
See Sport

Breakdown Assistance (Auto Repair)

Repair garages can be found everywhere in the city. It is advisable to contact the Hungarian Automobile Club (Magyar Autóklub, MAK) H-1024 Budapest II, Rómer Flóris u.4, tel: 666–404. The Hungarian Automobile Club maintains a breakdown service tel. 152-212 on eight major roads in Hungary (on the roads between Budapest and Balaton and Budapest and Hegyeshalom daily and on the other routes at week-ends). Members of foreign automobile clubs are only charged for spare parts.

Bus Stations

Buses to Transdanubia and abroad, and express buses to the airport.
Bus services to Vienna, Tatranská–Lomnica, Levice, Nitra, Galanta, Cluj and Tîrgu Mureş.
In the high season services to Munich, Venice, Rijeka and Opatija.

V, Engels tér

Buses to places east of the Danube.

XIV, Népstadion út

Buses to Zsambek.

I, Széna tér

Buses to Pilisvörösvár.

III, Obuda, Bécsi út

Buses to Monor.

IX, Nagyvárad tér

Buses to Erd.

XI, Kosztolányi tér

Buses to Vác

XIII, Bulcsu utca

Volán, V, Engels tér, tel: 172–562, 182–122.
Open weekdays from 6 a.m. to 6 p.m., Sat. to 4 p.m., closed Sun.

Information

Cafés, Espressos and Tea Shops

There are very many of these; the ones given here are those which are at present the most popular.

Astoria, V, Kossuth L. u. 19
Dunapark, XIII, Poszonyi út 38
*Gerbeaud, V, Vörösmarty tér 7

Coffee houses and cafés

Practical Information

*Hauer, VIII, Rákóczi út 49
Híd. V, Ferenc krt. 15
*Hungária (previously "New York"), VII, Lenin krt. 9–11
Korona, I, Disz tér 6
Különlegességi, VI, Népköztársaság útja 70
Müvész, VI, Népköztársaság útja 29
Nemzeti, VIII, József krt. 4
*Ruszwurm, I, Szentháromság u. 7

Espressos

*Angelika, I, Batthyány tér 7
Anna, V, Váci u. 7
Gyöngyszem, IX, Tolbuhin krt. 15
Omnia, VIII, Rákóczi út 67
Pálma, VII, Lenin krt. 36
Rákóczi, VII, Rákóczi út 40
Szimfónia, IX, Üllői út 65–67
Te + En, II, Bem rakpart 30

Tea shops

Rózsa, VIII, József Krt. 31b
Trojka, VI, Népköztársaság útja 28
Bajkal, V, Semmelweis u. 1–3

Camping Sites and Holiday Bungalows

Hárs-hegy, II, Hárshegy út 5–7, tel: 151–482.
Római Fürdő, III, Szentendrei út 189, tel: 686–260.
Strand Hotel, Csillahegy, III, Pusztakúti út 3, tel: 889–111.
Pap-sziget, on an island in the Danube near Szentendre.

There are more than 100 camp sites in Hungary, mainly open from May to September. Tourists can get information and reserve places in advance from the travel office of the Magyar Camping and Caravanning Club in Budapest, 6 Üllői út (tel. 336–563).

Car Rental

IBUSZ-AVIS
V, Martinelli tér 8, tel: 184–158.

Fótaxi – Rent-a-car
VII, Kertesz u. 24, tel: 221–471

Volántourist – Europcar, National IX, Vaskapu u. 16, tel: 334–783

Casino

Budapest Casino
Budapest Hilton Hotel, Hess András tér 1–3, tel: 868–859.
Baccarat, BlackJack, Boule, Roulette, slot machines.
Open: daily from 5 p.m.
Stakes are placed in West German marks. All hard currencies can be exchanged on the spot. Winnings are free of tax and can be freely taken out of Hungary.
Citizens of Socialist countries, except Yugoslavia, are not admitted.

Circus

Budapest has its own circus, the Fővárosi Nagycirkusz on the northern edge of the City Woodland Park (Városliget). In the modern circus building, erected in 1971, spectacular performances are given throughout the year (variety, performing animals, etc.).

Municipal Grand Circus

The Municipal Grand Circus (Fővárosi Nagycirkusz), Allatkerti körút 7, tel: 428–300.

Information and advance booking

Chemists (patika, gyóyszertár)

The address of the nearest chemist can be obtained from the reception desk at every hotel. Although Budapest has a great many chemists it may be difficult to find a particular medicine and it is preferable to bring your own particular medications.

VI, Lenin körút 95
VII, Rákóczi út 86

Chemists always open

Currency

The Hungarian monetary unit is the forint (Ft). One forint=100 fillérs. In circulation are banknotes in denominations of 10, 20, 50, 100 and 500 forints, coins worth 1, 2, 5, 10 forints and 10, 20 and 50 fillérs.

Currency

In Hungary, foreigners are not subjected to compulsory exchange of money. According to Hungarian law, foreign currency can only be exchanged at official bureaux de change – at the Hungarian National Bank (MNB), at branches of the Savings Bank (OTP), at travel agencies and tourist offices, at exchange offices in hotels and at camp sites. Changing money privately is strictly forbidden.

Changing money

Exchange rates are subject to fluctuation. The current rates are obtainable from banks, etc.

Exchange rates

In the larger hotels and restaurants and in some shops and stores, American Express, Bank of America, Carte Blanche, Diners Club, Eurocard, Interbanc, Access and Visa credit cards are accepted. Cash may be obtained from banks, bureaux de change, reception desks in the larger hotels and in most tourist offices (IBUSZ, Budapest Tourist, Volán, etc.). Eurocheques must be in West German marks.

Credit cards

Foreigners must declare their currency to the Customs officials. Hungarian currency can only be imported or exported in sums not exceeding 100 forints in coins only. Up to 50 per cent of Hungarian forints which have been exchanged for foreign currency can be exchanged back to a maximum value of $100 US at the following places: the frontier at Hegyeshalom, the

Currency regulations

Ferihegy Airport in Budapest, IBUSZ offices at the West and East Stations, and IBUSZ offices in the larger hotels.

Customs Regulations

Entry

Articles for use on the journey can be declared at the frontier. Gifts to the value of 5,000 forints per person (inland value) can be imported free. For gifts exceeding this value the Customs duty is 40 per cent. The import of pornographic material is not permitted.

Sporting guns and ammunition and radio apparatus, etc. can only be imported with a special permit.

Departure

Articles for use on the journey which have been brought in, may be taken out again without any necessary permit. Food for the journey, but for not more than three days may also be taken out. Tourists who have spent less than three days in Hungary are only allowed food for immediate consumption and not over 100 forints in value.

Gifts to the value of 3,000 forints (no one article to exceed 1,000 forints), but not gold, platinum, silver, museum articles, postage stamps, medicines, carpets, children's shoes, sausage, meat, bacon, sugar, flour and coffee, can be taken out.

Articles which have been bought in the Intertourist shops can be exported but the bill must be produced.

Information

Detailed and Current Customs regulations can be obtained before entry from Hungarian tourist offices or from IBUSZ representatives.

Electricity

In the city hotels, apparatus with European plugs can be used. Electricity in Budapest is supplied at 220 volts, 50 cycles AC. Adaptors are necessary for North American type plugs.

Embassies and Consulates (nagykovetseg; konzulatus)

Great Britain

Budapest V, Harmincad u. 6,
tel: 182–888

United States

Budapest V, Szabadság tér 12,
tel: 126–450

Canada

Budapest II, Budakeszi út 55/d,
tel: 165–858 or 165–949

Emergencies

Important telephone numbers:

Ambulance

tel: 04

Fire

tel: 05

Police

tel: 07

The State health service with all its institutions (district doctors, polyclinics, hospitals and their specialist ambulances) provides free first-aid for tourists. Foreign nationals can obtain out-patient treatment, for which there will be a charge.

Sickness

Events

Spring Festival (concerts, jazz, representational art)	March
Tourist Fair Freedom Festival on the Petőfi tér	15 March
International Fair Book week	May
Theatrum Szentendre	July
Constitution Day; parades, various performances on the Danube, evening firework display on Gellért Hill and on the bank of the Danube	20 August
Budapest Festival (concerts, art exhibitions, theatrical performances, pop) International Fair	September
Museum Month	October

First-Aid

tel: 04

Emergency

Basic first-aid treatment is free but a charge is made for further attention. Some doctors have private practices where treatment can be continued with payment.
Visitors should ensure that their insurance provides international cover.

Medical attention

See Chemists

Frontier Crossing Points

Road (open 24 hours a day)

Nickelsdorf–Hegyeshalom
Klingenbach–Sopron
Rattersdorf–Liebing–Köszeg
Schachendorf–Bucsu
Heiligenkreuz–Rábafüzes

Austria–Hungary

Rusovce–Rajka
Komarno–Komárom
Sahy–Parassapustza
Slovenské Darmety–Balassagyarmat

Czechoslovakia–Hungary

	Filakovo–Salgótarján
	Milhost–Tornyosnémeti
	Slovenské Nové Mesto–Sátoraljaújhely

Yugoslavia–Hungary	Hodos–Bajánsenye
	Dolga Vas–Rédics
	Gorican–Letenye
	Terezino Polje–Barcs
	Donji Miholjac–Drávaszabolcs
	Knezevo–Udvar
	Backi Breg–Hercegszántó
	Kelebia–Tompa
	Horgos–Röszke

| Soviet Union–Hungary | Tschop–Záhony |

Romania–Hungary	Bors–Artánd
	Varsand–Gyula
	Nadlac–Nagylak
	Petea–Csengersima

Rail (no visas issued)

Austria	Hegyeshalom, Sopron, Szentgotthárd
Czechoslavakia	Komárom, Szob, Hidasnémeti, Rajka, Sátoraljaujhely, Somos-köujfalu
Yugoslavia	Kelebia, Gyékényes, Murakeresztur, Magyarboly, Röszke
Soviet Union	Záhony
Romania	Biharkeresztes, Lökösháza, Nyirábrány, Kötegyan

Danube Ships

Budapest, Belgráde rakpart (issue of visas) also (without the issue of visas, only open during daylight): Györ, Komárom, Mohács, Szeged.

Airport

Budapest–Ferihegy (issue of visas)

Food and Drink

Dishes

Hungarian cuisine stresses, as does Austrian, dishes which include meat, flour or cereal, and great attention is paid to spices and other added ingredients. Old recipes which have been handed down are particularly prized and these are characterised by a liberal use of sour cream, lard and spices, especially paprika.

Some specialities:

Fried veal cutlet (Wiener Schnitzel).	Bécsi szelet
Veal fricassée with rice.	Borjúbecsinált rizzsel
Perch from Lake Balaton.	Fogas
Yeast buns with poppy seeds.	Guba
Well-spiced stew of beef, potato cubes, paprika, onions, tomatoes, garlic and caraway.	Gulyás (Gulasch)
A soup delicately spiced with hot paprika and often consisting of several kinds of fish (carp, catfish, etc.) with the addition of vegetables, onions, croûtons and sour cream.	Halászlé
Soup with liver dumplings.	Halleves majgomboccál
Baked catfish.	Harcsaszeletek roston
Plaited pastry.	Kalács
Layers of vegetables with sausage, bacon, minced meat, potatoes and slices of red pepper.	Koloszvári rakott káposzta
Soup with diced potatoes, croûtons, smoked bacon, tomatoes, slices of red pepper and herbs.	Lebbencs
Slices of red pepper in pork fat, steamed with tomatoes, onions and salt.	Lecsó
White cabbage prepared with a roux and sour cream and added bacon.	Lucskos káposzta
Noodles with poppy seed.	Mákos metélt
Eggs in aspic served with a fish salad.	Munkácsy
Pancakes.	Palacsinta
Onions, fat, herbs, paprika, meat, tomatoes, strips of red pepper, usually served with dumplings accompanying various meat dishes.	Paprikás
Chicken with paprika in pastry.	Paprikás csirke galuskával
Pastry cases filled with minced meat or finely chopped cabbage and baked.	Piroggen
Various kinds of pastry.	Pogatschen
Small pieces of meat braised in lard together with onions, paprika, garlic, carroway and marjoram.	Pörkölt
'Thieves bite' (various pieces of meat, bacon, potato and onion baked on a spit).	Rablóhús nyárson
Fried chicken.	Rántott csirke

Practical Information

Rétes	Sweet strudel usually filled with apples, nuts, poppy seeds, curd cheese or cherries.
Rigó jancsi	Chocolate cakes with jam.
Somlói galuska	Pieces of biscuit soaked in rum and served with cream.
Tokány	Stewed beef with a thick well-seasoned sauce.
Túróscsusza	Pasta dough with curd cheese and bacon.
Tüzdelt fácánsült	Larded pheasant.
Ujház tyúkleves	Boiling fowl in the Ujhaz manner (with vegetables, onions, garlic, mushrooms, parsley and vermicelli).
Vadas nyúl	Hare, 'hunter style'.
Zöldbableves	Soup with green beans.
Zöldborsó vajjal	Mange-tout peas prepared with butter.
Zsemlegombóccal	Bread dumplings.

Drinks

Wine (bor)

Wine has traditionally been produced in Hungary since Roman times. The most important Hungarian vineyards are in Sopron, Mór, Balaton, Eger, Tokaj, Szekszárd, Pecs, Vilány and Szeged. Their products can be sampled in numerous Budapest inns.

Favourite white wines:
Veltlini (Veltliner), Muskateli (Muscatel), Tramini (Traminer), Olazrizling (Italian Riesling), Rizling (Riesling), Szilváni (Silvaner), Szürkebarát (Grey Monk or Ruländer) and Furmint.

Popular red wines:
Bikavér ("Bull's Blood"), Kékfrankos (Blue Frankish), Leányka, Cabernet, Pinot Noir, Meriot.

Rosé wine:
Kadarka.

The wine label:
fehér=white; vörös=red; száras=dry; habzó=sparkling; édes=sweet;
kimert bor=vin ordinaire; asztali bor=table wine; minöségi bor=quality wine.

Tokay Wine:
The Furmint grape ripens well in the area of Tokay. Tokay is produced in three qualities: furmint (dry and light), szamorodni (mild and sweet), aszu (late vintage; with three, four or five stars; only in limited quantity).

Spirits

Hungarian fruit brandies are famous and popular, especially Barack (apricot brandy), Szilva (plum brandy) and, last but not least, cherry brandy.

As well as local beers, Yugoslavian and Austrian beers are becoming more and more popular in Budapest.
Connoisseurs of beer appreciate the Wernesgrüner, fresh from the barrel, which is imported from East Germany and is available in some inns.

Beer (sor)

Getting to Budapest

There are scheduled flights daily by British Airways and Malév from London to Budapest, either direct or via Rome or Frankfurt. From the USA and Canada visitors normally fly to Amsterdam, Copenhagen, Paris, Madrid or Vienna and continue on connecting flights to Budapest.

By air

The best service from the UK leaves Victoria Station in the morning and arrives at Budapest the following afternoon, via Dover, Ostend and Vienna. It is possible to change in Paris and continue on the Orient Express. An alternative route is via the Hook of Holland and Vienna.

By rail

Visitors taking their cars to Hungary are advised to travel on the German autobahns between Cologne and Munich to Salzburg and from there to Budapest. The AA in Great Britain and the AAA in the United States can provide further information.

By road

During the summer (May–September) there is a hydrofoil service on the Danube between Vienna, Bratislava and Budapest, the journey taking between four and five hours.

By boat

Horse-drawn Cabs (Fiacres)

In Buda and in Pest horse-drawn cabs have operated since the 18th c., just as in Vienna. After suffering from increasing competition from taxis, they have reappeared, especially in the castle quarter, as a tourist attraction.

Hospital

István kórház
IX, Nagyvárad tér 1, tel: 340–350

Important general hospitals

János kórház
XII, Diós árok 1, tel: 154–030

Margit kórhaz
III, Bécsi út 132, tel: 687–420

Semmelweis kórház
VIII, Gyulai Pál u. 2, tel: 342–180

Rescue Service Hospital
VI, Szobi u. 3, tel: 119–850

University Clinic
Üllői út, tel: 35–216

Practical Information

Inside Hotel Atrium Hyatt

Hotels (selection)

Categories
In most hotels a prior reservation is recommended. Budapest hotels are divided into four categories (1–5 stars). The 4- and 5-star hotels offer the same degree of comfort and service as luxury hotels of the same standard in Western countries. The 2- and 3-star hotels provide an acceptable standard and the hotels with 1 star should be considered as simple tourist hotels.

Prices
The prices of hotels in Budapest range from about £3/$4·80 for very simple accommodation to some £45/$72 per night for a single room in a 5-star hotel.

*****
*Atrium Hyatt, V, Roosevelt tér 2, 357 r.
*Duna Intercontinental, V, Apáczai Cs. J. u. 4, 350 r.
*Hilton, I, Hess A. tér 1–3, 323 r.
*Thermál, XIII, Margitsziget, 198 r.

****
Buda Penta, I, Krisztina krt. 41–43, 400 r.
Forum, V, Apáczai Cs. J. u. 12, 408 r.
*Gellért, XI, Szt. Gellért tér 1, 235 r.
Novotel Budapest, XII, Alkotás u. 63–67, 324 r.
Royal, VII, Lenin krt. 47–49, 366 r.
Olympia, XII, Eötvös u. 40, 173 r.

***
Aero, IX, Ferde u. 1–3, 139 r.
Budapest, II, Szilágyi E. fasor 47, 280 r.
Európa, II, Hárshegui u. 5–7, 163 r.
Flamenco, XI, Tass vezér u. 7, 326 r.

Grand Hotel Margitsziget, XIII, Margitsziget, 150 r.
Rege, II, Pálos u. 2, 80 r.
Stadion, XIV, Ifjúság útja 1–3, 348 r.
Szabadság, VII, Rákóczi út 90, 400 r.
Volga, XIII, Dózsa Gy. út 65, 313 r.

Astoria, V, Kossuth L. u. 19, 192 r.
Emke, VII, Akácfa u. 1–3, 70 r.
Expo, X, Dobi István út 10, 160 r.
Ifjúság, II, Zivatar u. 1–3, 100 r.
Metropol, VII, Rákóczi út 58, 102 r.
Nemzeti, VIII, József krt. 4, 69 r.
Palace, VIII, Rákóczi út 43, 113 r.
Park, VIII, Baross tér 10, 173 r.
Vénusz, III, Dósa u. 2–4, 73 r.
Vörös Csillag, XII, Rege u. 21, 41 r.
Wein, XI, Budaörsi út 88–90, 110 r.

Express, XII, Beethoven u. 7–9, 22 r.
Villa Pax Corporis, XI, Hársmajor u, 1, 20 r.

See Camping Sites and Holiday Bungalows   Holiday bungalows

Information

See Tourist Information

Language

Visitors will have little difficulty in making themselves   Foreign languages
understood in Budapest, for a knowledge of foreign languages
is a traditional part of general education, especially as
Hungarian is a language which is understood by relatively few
non-Hungarians and does not figure among the recognised
international languages. German is widely understood in
Hungary and many young people also speak quite good
English.

Hungarian belongs to the Finno-Ugrian family and therefore   Hungarian
has a special place in Europe. The varying pronunciation of
consonants and vowels will cause difficulty for the uninitiated.
In Hungarian the first syllable is the one always stressed.

Approximate equivalent in English
a=short open o (as in hot)   The alphabet and its
á=long a (as in calm)   pronunciation
c=ts (as in bits)
cs=ch (as in chat)
e=short e (as in bet)
é=long e (as the ai in fair)
gy=di (as adieu in French)
i=short i (as in bit)
í=long i (as the ee in breeze)
ly=sound of a voiced y (as in yes)
ny=gn (as in Cognac)
o=short o (as in cot)

Practical Information

ó=long o (as in mow)
ö=short o (as the e in the)
ô=long o (as the u in fur)
s=sh (as in show)
sz=sharp z (as in purse)
ty=ty (as the ch in chance)
u=short u (as in butter)
ú=long u (as the oo in boot)
ü=short u (as in hue)
û=long u (as in French tu)
v=v (as in very)
z=voiced z (as in buzz)
zs=voiced j (as in judge)

Numbers				
0	null, zéró, semmi	11	tizenegy	100 száz
1	egy	12	tizenkettô	200 kétszáz
2	kettô, két	20	húsz	1000 ezer
3	három	21	huszonegy	
4	négy	30	harminc	
5	öt	40	negyven	
6	hat	50	ötven	
7	hét	60	hatvan	
8	nyolc	70	hetven	
9	kilenc	80	nyolcvan	
10	tiz	90	kilencven	

Days of the week

Monday	hétfô	Friday	péntek
Tuesday	kedd	Saturday	szombat
Wednesday	szerda	Sunday	vasárnap
Thursday	csütörtök	Holiday	ünnep

Important words and phrases

accommodation	szállas
address	cim
airport	repülôgép
autumn	ôsz
bed	ágy
bill	számla
blue	kék
boat	csónak
bread	kenyér
bridge	hid
café	kávéház
castle	kastély
closed	zárva
day	nap
departure	indulás
diversion	terelôút
doctor	orvos
door	ajtó
early closing day	szimnap
east	kelet
embassy (consulate)	követség
emergency exit	vészkijárat
entrance	bejárat
evening	este
exchange	pénzváltás
exit	kijárat
express train	gyorsvonat
filling station	benzinkút

first-aid	elsősegély
free	szabad
frontier	határ
German	németül
Good bye	viszontlatasra
Good day	jó napot
Good evening	jó estét
Good morning	jóreggelt
help, assistance	segitség
hill	domb
hour, clock	óra
How much?	mennyi?
How much is that?	mennyibe kerül?
Hungary	Magyarország
I (don't) understand	(nem) értem
information	információ, felvilágositás
inn	vendéglő
island	sziget
lake, pond	tó
left	balra
letter	lévél
look out!	vigyázat!
luggage	poggyász
Madam (addressing a lady)	asszony
May I?	megengedi?
milk	tej
name	név
night	éjszaka
no parking	várakozni tilos!
north	észak
pardon	pardon!
pâtisserie	cukrászada
play street	játszóutca
please	kérem
police	rendőrség
post office	Posta
prohibited	tilos!
railway	vasút
red	piros
restaurant	etterem
right	jobbra
road, street	utca, út
road works	útjavitás
room	szoba
shop, store	aruház
Sir (addressing a gentleman)	úr
south	dél
spring	tavasz
station	állomás, pályaudvár
storey	emelet
summer	nyár
telegram	távirat
Thank you	köszönöm
tip	borravaló
toilet (gentlemen)	urak
toilet (ladies)	nők
town	város
tram	villamos
water	víz
weather	időjárás

149

week	hét
west	nyugat
What is that?	mi ez?
When?	mikor?
Where?	hol?
white	fehér
wine bar	borozó
wine vault	borpince
winter	tél
village	falu
year	év
yellow	sárga
yesterday	tegnap

Lost Property Offices

Foreigners' Department KEOKH
VI, Rudas László u. 45
Mon. 8.30 a.m.–4.30 p.m., Tues. – Fri. 8.30 a.m.–12 noon

Central Office
V, Engels tér 5, tel: 174–961
Mon. 8 a.m.–6 p.m., Tues.–Thurs. 8 a.m.–5 p.m., Fri 8 a.m.–
3 p.m.

Office of the Budapest Transport Authority (BKV)
VII, Akácfa u. 18, tel: 226–613
Mon., Tues., Thurs., 7 a.m.–4 p.m., Wed., Fri. 7 a.m.–6.30 p.m.

Museums

Opening times | Budapest museums are generally open Tues.–Sun. between 10 a.m. and 6 p.m.

Entrance fee | Some museums make an entrance charge (between 5 and 15 Ft).

List of museums | Agricultural Museum (Mezógazdasági Múzeum)
See A–Z, City Woodland Park

Art Gallery (Múcsarnok)
See A–Z, Heroes' Square

Arts and Crafts Museum (Iparmúveszeti Múzeum)
See A–Z, Arts and Crafts Museum

Aquincum (Archaeological Museum)
See A–Z, Obuda

Béla Bartók House (Bartók Béla Emlekház)
II, Csalán u. 29

Castle Museum, Historical Museum (Történeti Múzeum)
See A–Z, Castle Palace

Castle Museum Nagytétény (Nagytétény Kastély-múzeum)
See A Z, Nagytétény

China Museum (Kina-múzeum)
See A–Z, China Museum

Church Museum (Matthias Church)
See A–Z Matthias Church

Commerce and Catering Museum
(Kereskedelmi és Vendéglátóipari Múzeum) See A–Z, Buda,
Important Streets and Squares,
Fortuna utca

Contra Aquincum
See A–Z, Március 15 tér

Ernst Museum (Ernst Múzeum)
See A–Z, Nagymező utca

Ethnographical Museum (Néprajzi Múzeum)
See A–Z, Ethnographical Museum

Evangelical Provincial Museum
(Evangélikus Országos Múzeum)
See A–Z, Inner Ring, Deák Ferenc tér

Ferenc Hopp Museum for East Asian Art
(Hopp Ferenc Kelet-ázsiai Művészeti Múzeum)
See A–Z, Ferenc Hopp Museum for East Asian Art

Fire Brigade Museum (Tűzoltó-múzeum)
See A–Z, Kőbánya

Foundry Museum (Öntödei Múzeum)
See A–Z, Viziváros

Jewish Museum
(Országos Zsidó Vallási és Történeti Gyűjtemény)
See A–Z, Pester Synagogue

Kiscelli Museum (Kiscelli Múzeum)
See A–Z, Obuda

Local History Museum Obuda
(Obuda Helytörténeti Múzeum)
III, Fő tér

Military History Museum (Hadtörténeti Múzeum)
See A–Z, Buda, Important Streets and Squares,
Kapisztrán tér

Museum of Fine Arts (Szépművészeti Múzeum)
See A–Z, Museum of Fine Arts

Museum of the Hungarian Workers' Movement
(Magyar Munkásmozgalmi Múzeum)
See A–Z, Castle Palace

National Gallery (Nemzeti Galéria)
See A–Z, Castle Palace

National Museum (Nemzeti Múzeum)
See A–Z, National Museum

Natural History Museum
(Természettudományi Múzeum)
VIII, Baross u. 13

Open Air Museum Szentendre (Skanzen)
See A–Z, Szentendre

Petőfi Museum (Petőfi Múzeum)
See A–Z, Petőfi Muzeum

Pharmaceutical Museum "Golden Eagle"
(Arany Sas Patika-múzeum)
See A–Z, Buda, Important Streets and Squares,
Tárnok utca

Postage Stamp Museum (Bélyeg-múzeum)
VII, Hársfa u. 47

Postal Museum (Posta Múzeum)
See A–Z, Népköztarsaság útja

Roman Military Town (Táborvárosi Múzeum)
See A–Z, Obuda

Semmelweis Museum (Semmelweis Múzeum)
See A–Z, Tabán

Transport Museum (Közlekedési Múzeum)
See A–Z, City Woodland Park

Underground Railway Museum (Földalatti Vasúti Múzeum)
See A–Z, Inner Ring, Deák Ferenc tér

Music

Concert halls

Franz List Academy of Music
VI, Liszt Ferenc tér 8

Vigadó
V, Vigadó tér

Buda Redoubt
I, Corvin tér 8

Matthias Church
I, Szentharomság tér

Reformed Church
V, Kálvin tér

Zichy Castle
II, Fő tér 1

State Opera House
VI, Nepköztársaság útja 22

Opera

Tourist Information, tel: 179–800

Programme of events

Philharmonia,
V Vörösmarty tér 1
tel: 176–222

Advance booking

Newspapers and Magazines

It is possible to buy some Western newspapers and magazines in shops and in the major hotels. The newspapers *The Times*, *The International Herald Tribune* (Paris edition) and the weekly *Time* and *Newsweek* magazines are available the day after their publication.

International press

A bilingual English-German paper, *The Daily News – Neueste Nachrichten*, is published by the Hungarian news agency MTI and is widely available. There is also a free monthly magazine *Coming Events in Hungary* also with text in English and German and additionally in French. A new Hungarian quarterly in English deals with Hungarian life, culture and politics.

English-language publications

Night-life

There are cabarets in several of the leading hotels and also at:

*Maxim, VII, Akácfa u.3, tel: 420–145,
variety programme, changing monthly

Selection

*Moulin Rouge, VI, Nagymezö u. 17, tel: 124–492,
variety programme, changing frequently

Casanova, I, Batthyány tér 4, tel: 388–756

Fekete Macska, IX, Knézits u. 1, tel: 170–469, 7 p.m.–3 a.m.

Pipacs-Bar, V, Aranykéz u. 15, tel: 185–505

Opening times

Mon.–Fri. 7 a.m.–7 p.m., Sat. 10 a.m.–2 p.m.

Food shops

Mon.–Fri. 10 a.m–6 p.m., Sat. 10 a.m.–2 p.m.

Stores

Mon.–Thurs. 8 a.m.–5 p.m., Fri. 8 a.m.–2 p.m.

Banks

Mon.–Fri. 8 a.m.–7 p.m., Sat. 8 a.m.–12 noon

Post offices

Usually Tues.–Sun. 10 a.m.–6 p.m.

Museums

Opera

See Music
See Theatre

Photography (fénykép)

Prohibited	Photographing and filming military and industrial areas, airports, railway stations, bridges and radio stations is forbidden. In frontier areas and shops there is an absolute ban on photography.
Permitted	Except for the information given above anything in Hungary may be photographed and filmed for private use. Photographs and films intended for commercial use must be declared to the Pressinform Office. Permission from the appropriate authority should be sought before photographing industrial, agricultural or administrative installations. An individual's permission should be obtained before he or she is photographed.
Film material	It is advisable to bring films, etc. in sufficient quantity with you since Western miniature and super-8 films can only be obtained in a few shops.

Post (posta)

Main Post Office	V, Petőfi Sándor utca 13–15 Opening times: Mon.–Sat. 7 a.m.–9 p.m., Sun. and holidays 8 a.m.–1 p.m.
Post offices open 24 hours a day	Keleti pályaudvar (East Station) VII, Verseny utca 1
	Nyugati pályaudvar (West Station) VI, Lenin körút 105
Poste restante	Magyar Posta (Main Post Office) H-1052 Budapest V, Petőfi Sándor utca 13–15
Long-distance Telephone, Telegrams, Telex	Annex of Main Post Office V, Petőfi Sándor utca 17–19 Opening times: Mon.–Sat. 7 a.m.–9 p.m., Sun. and holidays 8 a.m.– 1 p.m.
Telegrams by phone	tel: 02
Telephone	See Telephone

Public Holidays

New Year	1 January

A Budapest tram

Excursion, ship on the Danube

Liberation Day	4 April
Easter Monday	March/April
Labour Day	1 May
Constitution Day	20 August
Anniversary of the Great October Socialist Revolution	7 November
Christmas	25–26 December

Public Transport

Public transport is provided by trams, trolleybuses, buses and the Underground (Metro). Bus

Trams, trolleybuses and the Underground operate generally between 4 a.m. and midnight and on a few main routes throughout the night. A new ticket must be used when changing from one vehicle to another. Buses operate in general between 5 a.m. and 11 p.m. Tickets are only valid for one journey. The yellow tram and trolleybus tickets, as well as the blue bus tickets, must be obtained in advance from tobacconists or at the ticket offices at the various terminals. No tickets can be bought on the vehicles. Tickets have to be cancelled by the passenger in a machine on the vehicle.

The cog-wheel railway on the Szabadság-hegy, the chair-lift Rail on the János-hegy, the funicular on Castle Hill and the local boats on the Danube are also under the control of the Budapest Transport Authority.

Radio (Magyar Rádió és Televizió, MRT)

There are brief bulletins in English broadcast on Budapest radio and TV. There are two television channels and on Channel 2 imported programmes can sometimes be seen, either in the original language or with English sub-titles.

Railway Stations

Josephtown Station (Józsefvárosi pályaudvar)	Internal traffic to Nagykáta–Szolnok and Kunszentmiklós –Tass–Kiskunhalas.
East Station (Keleti pályaudvar)	Trains to Austria, Switzerland, West Germany, France, Belgium and Holland. Trains to Romania, USSR, Yugoslavia, Bulgaria, Czechoslovakia, East Germany and Poland. Internal traffic to Miskólc and Békéscsaba.
South Station (Déli pályaudvar)	Trains to Austria and Yugoslavia. Regional traffic to the Velence Lake and to Lake Balaton. Internal traffic to Pécs, Nagykanizsa, Tapolca, Szombathely and Győr.
West Station (Nyugati pályaudvar)	Trains to Romania, Czechoslovakia and East Germany. Internal traffic to Debrecen, Nyíregyháza, Szeged, Lajosmizse and Veresegyháza.

Restaurants (selection)

Note	Hot meals are obtainable until quite late where indicated. On the days named the restaurants are usually closed. In many restaurants there is gipsy or Viennese music.
First-class restaurants	*Fortuna, I, Hess Andras tér 4, tel: 161–411 *Gundel, XIV, Allatkerti út 2, tel: 221–002, noon–4 p.m., 7 p.m.–midnight *Régi Országház, I, Országház u. 17, tel: 160–225, until 1 a.m. *Százéves, V, Pesti Barnabás u. 2, tel: 183–608
Speciality restaurants	Aranyfácán, XII, Szilágyi Erzsébet fasor 33, tel: 151–001 Aranyszarvas, I, Szarvas tér 1, tel: 351–305, until 1 a.m. (game) Bajkál, V, Semmelweis u. 1–3, tel: 176–839 (specialities from the Soviet Union) Berlin, V, Szt. István krt. 13, tel: 316–533, until midnight (Berlin cuisine) Bukarest, XI, Bartók Béla út 48, tel: 252–203, until 5 a.m. (Romanian cuisine) Csárda Potyka, VIII, Népszinház u. 23, tel: 340–962 (fish dishes)

Restaurant with Gipsy music

Etoile, XIII, Pozsonyi út 4, tel: 122–242, until midnight; Sun.
(French cuisine)
Góbé, VIII, József krt. 28, tel: 341–711 (lamb specialities)
Hársfa, II, Vörös Hadsereg útja 132, tel: 164–002 (game)
Karczma Polska, XII, Márvány u. 19, tel: 151–069 (Polish
cuisine)
Kislugas, II, Szilágyi Erzsébet fasor 77, tel: 351–503 (Serbian
cuisine)
Lúdas, IX, Tolbuhin krt. 15, tel: 176–712 until 10 p.m. (goose
dishes)
Matrózcsárda, IX, Alsórakpart, tel: 182–305, until midnight
(fish dishes)
Megyeri Csárda, IV, Váci út 102, tel: 693–964, until midnight
(fish dishes)
Napoletana, V, Petöfi tér, tel: 185–714, until midnight; Mon.
(Italian cuisine)
˚Nimród, V, Münnich Ferenc u. 24, tel: 116–098 (game)
Öreghalász, IV, Árpád u. 20, tel: 694–192, until midnight (fish
dishes)
˚Sipos, III, Lajos u. 46, tel: 686–480 (fish dishes)
Szeged, XI, Bartók Béla út 1, tel: 666–503, until 1 p.m. (fish
dishes)
Szerb, V, Nagy Ignác u. 16, tel: 111–858 (Serbian cuisine)
Szófia, V, Kossuth Lajos tér 13–15, tel: 118–232 (Bulgarian
cuisine)
Tabáni Kakas, I, Attila út 27, tel: 352–139, until midnight; Sun.
(poultry)
Vadászkert, XIV, Erzsébet királyne útja 5, tel: 636–399, until
midnight (game)

Practical Information

A Vörös Postakocsihoz, IX, Ráday út 15, tel: 176–756, until
11 p.m. (dishes from the turn of the century)
Vörös Sárkány, VI, Népköztársaság útja 80, tel: 318–757, until
midnight (Chinese cuisine)

Restaurants with Hungarian cuisine

Arok, XIV, Nagy Lajos király útja 64, tel: 633–040, until 11 p.m.
Borkatakomba, XXII, Nagytétényi út 64, tel: 464–859, until
midnight; Tues.
Csiki, IX, Angyal u. 37, tel: 136–627, until 11 p.m.
Emke Kalocsa, VII, Lenin krt. 2, tel. 220–689
Ezerjó, XIV, Városliget, Allatkerti krt. 3, tel: 428–502, until
midnight
*Mátyás Pince (old well-known Matthias cellar), Március 15
tér, 7, tel: 181–693, until 1 a.m.
Ménes Csárda, V, Apáczi Csere J. u. 15, tel: 170–803, until
midnight
*Nótafa, XIX, Ady Endre út 37, tel: 272–634, until midnight
Thököly, XIX, Thököly út 80, tel: 225–444

Restaurants with international cuisine

Abbázia, VI, Népköztársaság útja 49, tel: 224–624
Apostolok, V, Kígyó u. 4–6, tel: 183–704, until midnight
Aranyhordó, I, Tárnok u. 16, tel: 361–399, until midnight
Aranykacsa, XIV, Örs vezér tere 2, tel: 630–821, until midnight
Aranykakas, IV, Pozsonyi úti ltp. U ép. 111, tel: 694–132, until
11 p.m.
Baross, VIII, József krt. 45, tel: 138–402, until midnight
Bástya, VIII, Rákóczi út 29, tel: 130–477, until 11 p.m.
Erzsébet, VII, Lenin krt. 48, tel: 222–040, until 1 a.m.
Európa, II, Mártirok útja 43–45, tel: 158–665, until 3 a.m.
Ezüstsirály, IX, Napfény u. 7., tel: 471–352, until 11 p.m.
Gresham, V, Roosevelt tér 5, tel: 172–407, until 11 p.m.
*Gyertya, VI, Bajcsy-Zsilinszky út 21, tel: 121–039, until 4 a.m.
Harsfa, II, Vörös Hadsereg útja 132, tel: 164–002, until
midnight
Hid, IX, Ferenc krt. 17, tel. 337–994, until 11 p.m.
*Hungária, VII, Lenin krt. 9–11, tel: 221–648, until 10 p.m.
Kárpátia, V, Károlyi M. u. 4–8, tel: 173–596
Kiskakukk, XIII, Pozsonyi út 12, tel: 321–732
Lucullus, VII, Lenin krt. 7, tel: 420–398, until 11 p.m.
Lúdlab, VII, Lenin krt. 39, tel: 423–120, until 4 p.m.; Sun.
Margitkert, II, Margit u. 15, tel: 354–791, until midnight
Márványmenyasszony, I, Márvány u. 6, tel: 151–229, until
1 a.m.
Megálló, VII, Tancs krt. 23, tel: 223–015
Múzeum, VIII, Múzeum krt. 12, tel: 138–891
*Müvész, XIII, Vigszinház u. 5., tel: 110–235
Postakocsi, III, Fö tér 2, tel: 351–159, until 2 p.m.
Rákóczi, VIII, Rákóczi út 55, tel: 145–775
Rozsa, IV, Titó út 20–22, tel: 695–138, until midnight
Vadrózsa, II, Pentelei M. u. 15, tel: 351–118, until midnight
Vasmacska, III, Laktanya u. 3–5, tel: 887–123, until 1 a.m.

Beer parlours

Berlini szuszterinas, VIII, József krt. 31a, tel: 138–226
Bécsi, V, Eötvös u. 8, tel: 174–504
Borsod, V, Honvéd u. 18, tel: 111–856
Erzsébet, VII, Lenin krt. 48, tel: 223–003
Hági, VII, Huszár u. 7, tel: 421–565
Krisztina, XII, Krisztina krt. 25, tel: 363–024
Krúdy, IV, Gyula u. 19, tel: 131–254
Montmartre, VI, Népköztársaság útja 47, tel: 224–610

A két Medvéhez, IX, Üllöi út 45, tel: 130–282, until 11 p.m.
Trojka, VI, Népköztársaság útja 28, tel: 124–688
Tükövy, V, Rosenberg házaspár u. 15, tel: 311–931, until
midnight
Wernesgrüner Bierstube, II, Bem rakpart 49

Háry, VIII, Bródy Sándor u. 30a, tel: 341–989   Wine bars
Kékfrankos, VI, Liszt Ferenc tér 7, tel: 421–582
Lövér, VI, Majakovszkij u. 100
Rondella, V, Régiposta u. 4, tel: 183–503
Taverna, V, Szabadsajtó út, tel: 182–404

See Hotels   Hotel restaurants

See Cafés, Espressos, Tea Shops   Coffee shops

Sailing (on Lake Balaton)

Sailing on Lake Balaton is very popular either in one's own boat
or in boats which can be hired on the lake (in Siófok,
Balatonfüred, Keszthely and other places).
For large yachts one needs the sail indicator 'A'. Visitors who
bring their own yachts to Hungary need a triptyque (carnet).
This triptyque can be obtained from the national Automobile
Clubs.
Since January 1976 motorboats have been banned from Lake
Balaton but sailing boats with auxiliary motors are allowed.
There are mooring-places for small boats on Lake Balaton in
the vicinity of the hotels and bungalow complexes. Larger
boats must tie up at Balatonfüred near the hotels Marina and
Annabella, in Tihany near the sailing club, in Balatonalmádi at
the sailing club and in Keszthely near the hotel Helikon boats'
slipway: very large boats in Balatonfüred, Siófok and in Tihany,
Keszthely.

Ship/Boat Services

Danube

International Landing-stage (Danube Passenger Ships)   Landing-stages
V, Balgrád rakpart, tel: 181–758

Landing-stage for excursion ships and local services
V, Vigadó tér, tel: 181–223

From Budapest, landing-stage Vigadó tér, in the high season   Excursions
excursions are operated daily (at other times only at week-ends
and holidays) to Viségrad and Esztergom (see Danube Bend)

MAHART   Information
V, Apáczai Csere János u. 11, tel: 181–880
V, Vigadó tér, tel: 181–223
I, Bem József tér, tel: 354–907

See Getting to Budapest, by ship
See Travel Agents

Lake Balaton

Ferries	Between the peninsula of Tihany (north bank) and Szántód (south bank) there are frequent car and passenger ferries.
Excursions	During the high season excursions operate from all the important holiday centres. Small craft link all the larger places with a regular service. Sometimes evening excursions with dancing and entertainment are available.
Information	See Travel Agents

Shopping

Although Budapest cannot be compared as a shopping centre with London, Munich, Milan or Paris, nevertheless the Hungarian capital offers the most comprehensive assortment of goods in eastern Europe. The main shopping streets are Váci utca, Kossuth Lajos utca, Rákóczi út, Múzeum körút, Tolbuhin körút, Kigjo Ut, Petofi Ut, Sandor Ut and Népköztársaság útja, as well as the streets in the Castle district.

Souvenirs

In all tourist centres, souvenirs of various qualities are on offer. Highly original gifts, in addition to the Rubic Cube, are handmade textiles (blouses, dresses, tablecloths, pillow-slips, etc) which are quite often magnificently embroidered. Kalocsaer blouses, Matyó embroidery, jackets with felt decoration and woven rural articles are popular, as are Herend porcelain, Pecser china, pottery from Siebenburgen or carved wooden cutlery and vessels of the Puszta herdsmen tradition. Glassware, leather goods (especially elegant ladies' handbags), shoes, ties, belts and natural medicaments (pollen from blossoms, propolis, honey and medicinal herbs) are popular with tourists due to their relatively favourable prices.

Records made in Budapest studios of music by the famous Hungarian composers Bartók, Kodály, Goldmark and Liszt are always well worth buying, as are books and old prints which can often be found at reasonable prices in the local antiquarian shops.

The most sought after Budapest souvenirs are Hungarian salami, Barack (apricot brandy), Szilva (plum brandy), Tokay (dessert wine) and paprika of all kinds.

Spa Establishments (Gyógyfürdő)

Budapest

Springs	The richest mineral springs in Europe are to be found in the area of the city of Budapest – 123 registered thermal springs service no less than 32 baths of which 9 are officially recognised as

spas. The most productive, which reach up to 76 °C (160 °F), arise along a geological fault which stretches from Gellért Hill (Gellért-hegy) northwards right out over Margaret Island.

*Gallért   Baths
XI, Kelenhegyi út
Treatment includes: thermal, steam, wave and other baths, mud packs, massage, gymnastics, physio- and electro-therapy, sauna, solarium, etc.
Opening times: steam and normal baths Mon–Fri. 6.30 a.m.– 7 p.m., Sat. 6.30 a.m.–noon; wave baths and other treatments: daily 6 a.m.–7 p.m.

*Széchenyi
XIV, Allatkerti út 11
Treatment includes; thermal, wave and other baths, mud packs, massage, gymnastics, physio-therapy, solarium, sauna, drinking fountain, etc.
Opening times: thermal and normal baths Mon.–Fri. 6.30 a.m.–7 p.m., Sun. 6.30 a.m.–noon; swimming-bath daily 6 a.m.–6 p.m.; sauna Mon.–Sat. 6 a.m.–6 p.m., drinking fountain daily 7 a.m.–6.30 p.m.

*Lukács
II, Frankel Leó út 26–29
Treatment includes: thermal, steam and mud baths, massage, therapeutic gymnastics, physio- and electro-therapy, drinking cures, etc.
Opening times: steam and normal baths Mon.–Fri. 6.30 a.m.– 8p.m., Sat. and Sun. 6.30 a.m.–1 p.m.; mud baths Mon.–Fri. 6.30 a.m.–8 p.m., Sat. 6.30 a.m.–2 p.m.; wave bath Mon.–Sat. 6 a.m.–8 p.m., Sun. 6 a.m.–5 p.m.; drinking fountain Mon.–Sat. 6 a.m.–7 p.m., Sun. 6 a.m.–noon.

Rudas
I, Döbrentei tér 9
Treatment includes: thermal, steam and other baths, irrigation, massage, physio- and electro-therapy, drinking fountain.
Opening times: steam and normal baths Mon–Fri. 6 a.m.– 8p.m., Sat. 6 a.m.–1 p.m., Sun. 6 a.m.–noon; wave bath Mon.–Fri. 6 a.m.–6 p.m., Sat. 6 a.m.–8 p.m., Sun. 6 a.m.–noon; drinking fountain Mon.–Sat. 6 a.m.–7 p.m.

Rác
I Hadnagy u. 8–10
Treatment includes: thermal and other baths, massage, conditioning, solarium.
Opening times: baths Mon.–Sat. 6.30 a.m.–7 p.m.

Király
II, Fó utca 84
Treatment includes: thermal, steam and other baths, massage, sauna.
Opening times: Mon.–Sat. 6.30 a.m.–7 p.m.

Dandár
IX, Dandár u. 5
Treatment includes: thermal, steam and other baths, massage.
Opening times: Mon.–Fri. 7 a.m.–7 p.m., Sat. 7 a.m.–1 p.m., Sun. 6.30 a.m.–1 p.m.

Pesterzsébet
XX, Csepeli átjáró 1
Treatment includes: thermal, steam and other baths, massage.
Opening times: Mon.–Sat. 7 a.m.–7 p.m.

*Hotel Thermál, Margaret Island
XIII, Margitsziget
Treatment includes: thermal and other baths, massage, mud packs, physio- and electro-therapy, gymnastics, irrigation, sauna, etc.
Opening times: for hotel guests daily 7 a.m.–9 p.m., for outpatients 7 a.m.–7 p.m.

Lake Balaton and district

*Balatonfüred (north bank of Lake Balaton)
Treatment includes: carbonic and sulphur baths, mud packs, massage.
Information: Balantontourist-Nord, Balatonfüred, Blaha Lujza u. 5, tel: 40–281.

*Héviz
5 km (3 miles) north-west of Keszthely (west end of Balaton)
Treatment includes: remedial bathing, gymnastics, electro-therapy, therapeutic mud.
Information: Balantontourist-Nord, Winterbad, Héviz, tel: 11–048

Dental treatment

In the Kurhotel, Thermal, Budapest and in Héviz, near Lake Balaton, moderately priced accommodation is available for visitors seeking dental treatment.

Sport

Stadiums

Népstadion
XIV, Istvánmezei út 1–3

Kisstadion
Szabó József utca 1
nearby is the Millenaris Sportsground (Millenáris sportpálya)

Horse-racing tracks

Trotting race-track (Ügető-pálya)
VIII, Kerepesi út 9

Racetrack (Lóverseny tér galopp-pálya)
X, Dobi István utca 2

Tennis-courts

Margitszieget tenispálya
XIII, Margaret Island

Varosmajor teniszpálya
II, Varosmajor

Sports hall

Sportcsarnok
(Sports Hall "Budapest")
XIV, Istvánmezei út 1–3

New "Budapest" sports hall

Müjegpálya XIV, Városliget	Artificial ice-rink
Gellért XI, Kelenhegyi út 4	Open all year covered and open-air swimming-pools

Hajós Alfréd sportuszoda
XIII, Margaret Island

Komjádi Béla sportuszoda
II, Komjádi Béla utca 2–4

Csillahegyi
III, Pusztakúti u. 3

Lukács
II, Frankel Leó u. 25–29

Rudas
I, Döbrentei tér 9

Szabadság
XIII, Népfürdő u. 30

Széchenyi
XIV, Allatkerti körút 11

Ujpesti
IV, Arpád út 114–120

Practical Information

Open May–Sept. open-air swimming-pools	Cinkotai XVI, Allomás tér 1
	Csepeli XXI, Hollandi út
	Albertfalvai XI, Szabadság út 84
	Kispesti XIX, Ady Endre út 99
	Pesterzsébet XX, Csepeli átjáró
	Pestlőrinc XVIII, Vörös Hadsereg útja 180
	Pünkösdfürdő III, Vörös Hadsereg útja 272
	Palatinus XIII, Margaret Island
	Rákoscsabai XVII, Kelecsényi út
	Római III, Lőpormalom dűlő
Spas	See entry
Winter sports	Ski-lift János-hegy Downhill ski-run Normafa Ski-jump Jánas-hegy Artificial and natural ice-rinks in Városliget

Taxis

In Budapest taxis can be ordered by dialling 222–222 (FŐTAXI) or 666–666 (VOLANTAXI). Taxis can be ordered in advance by dialling 188–888. They are clearly identified by the sign TAXI. At the beginning of the journey the taxi meter shows the basic fare which is 8 forints; after each 500 metres ($\frac{3}{10}$ mile) the fare rises by 2 forints.

Car Rental	See entry

Telegrams

See Post
See Telephone

Telephone

A local call (from 7 a.m. to 6 p.m. 3 minutes; from 6 p.m. to
7 a.m. 6 minutes) costs 1.5 forints (from coin operated boxes
a 2-forint coin)

Local calls

Calls can be dialled directly in Budapest including calls made
from many coin-operated boxes (minimum 10 forints; follow
the instructions carefully).

Dialled calls

Great Britain: 0044
United States and Canada: 001

International dialling codes

tel: 172–200

Information for long-
distance calls in English and
other foreign languages

tel: 09

Telephone exchange for
international calls

Annex of Main Post Office
V, Petőfi Sándor utca 17–19
Opening times: Mon.–Sat. 7 a.m.–9 p.m., Sun. and holidays
8 a.m.–1 p.m.

Long-distance call office

tel: 02

Telegrams

See entry

Post

Theatres

Arena Theatre (Körszínhaz)
XIV, Városliget, tel: 224–251

Addresses

Atila-József Theatre (József Attila Színház)
XIII, Váci út 63, tel: 208–238

Castle Theatre (Várszínház)
I, Szinház utca 1–3, tel: 868–664

Children's Theatre (Gyermekszínház)
VI, Paulay Ede utca 35, tel: 224–495

Civic Operetta Theatre
Fővárosi Operett Szinház)
VI, Nagymező utca 17, tel: 126–470

Erkel Theatre (Erkel Színház)
VIII, Köztarsaság tér 30, tel: 330–540

Josephtown Theatre (Józsefvárosi Színház)
VIII, Kulich Gyula tér 6, tel: 338–620

József-Katona Theatre (Katona József Színház)
V, Petőfi Sándor utca 6, tel: 186–559

Practical Information

Literary Theatre Miklós Radnóti
(Radnóti Miklós Irodalmi Színpad)
VI, Nagymező utca 11, tel: 420–561

Madách Studio Theatre (Madách-Kamaraszínház)
VII, Madách tér 6, tel: 226–422

Madách Theatre (Madách Színház)
VII, Lenin körút 29–33, tel: 220–677

Microscope Theatre (Mikroszkóp színpad)
VI, Nagymező utca 22–24, tel: 113–322

National Theatre (Nemzéti színház)
VII, Hevesi Sándor tér 2, tel: 413–849

Odry Theatre (Odry színpad)
VIII, Vas utca 2, tel: 337–503

Old Theatre (Játékszin)
VI, Lenin körút 106, tel: 120–430

Opera House (Magyar Allami Operaház)
VI, Népköztarsaság útja 22, tel: 320–126

Pest Theatre (Pesti Színház)
V, Váci utca 9, tel: 185–547

Puppet Theatre (Allami Bábszinház)
VI, Népköztarsaság útja 69,
tel: 422–702

Thalia Theatre (Thalia Színház)
VI, Nagymező utca 22–24, tel: 310–500

Theatre of Comedy (Vigszínház)
XIII, Szent István körút 14, tel: 110–430

University Theatre (Egyetemi Színpad)
V, Pesti Barnabás utca 1, tel: 183–311

Variety Theatre (Vidám Színpad)
VI, Révay utca 18, tel: 311–311

Advance booking

Theatre box offices are normally open on Thurs.–Sat. 3–5 p.m.
The following advance booking offices are open during normal business hours:
VI, Népköztarsaság útja 18, tel: 120–100
II, Moszkva tér 3, tel: 359–136
V, Vörösmarty tér 1, tel: 176–222

Advance programme information

Tourinform, tel: 179–800
Mon.–Fri. 7 a.m.–9 p.m., Sat. 7 a.m.–8 p.m., Sun. 8 a.m.–1 p.m.

Newspapers

See entry

Time

Hungary observes Central European Time (Greenwich Mean Time + 1 hour); in summer Central European Summer Time (Daylight Saving) (Greenwich Mean Time + 2 hours)

Tourist Information

The most important addresses for information concerning a proposed tour of Budapest are the IBUSZ Bureaux:

Hungarian State Travel Bureaux IBUSZ

Danube Travel Limited, Central Agent IBUSZ Hungary, 6 Conduit Street, London W1R 9TG, tel: (01) 493 0263.

Great Britain

IBUSZ Hungarian Travel Ltd, Suite 520, 630 Fifth Avenue, Rockefeller Center, New York, NY 10020 tel: (212) 582 7412; toll free 800/367–7878.

United States

Tourinform, H-1051 Budapest V, Petőfi Sándor u. 17–19, tel: 179–800. IBUSZ, H-1364 Budapest V, Felszabadulás tér 1, tel: 186–866. Budapest Tourist, H-1051 Budapest V, Roosevelt tér 5, tel: 173–555.

Budapest

See entry

Travel agents

Traffic Regulations

International driving permit is not obligatory but a national driving licence and registration document should be taken.

Vehicle documents

Vehicles must display an oval nationality plate.

Nationality plate

In Hungary accidents must be reported if possible within 24 hours, but at the latest on the next working day to the relevant authority which, in Budapest, is the Department of International Motor Insurance of the State Insurance Company (AB, Budapest XI, Hamzsabégi út 60, tel: 669–755); elsewhere in Hungary it is the branch offices of the State Insurance Company.

Vehicle insurance

The wearing of seat belts in the front seats is compulsory.

Seat belts

Children under six years of age may not travel in front seats.

Children

In Hungary it is an offence to drive after drinking any alcohol.

Alcohol ban

Vehicles travel on the right. In built-up areas: cars 60 km/h (37 mph), buses, cars with trailers and motor cycles 50 km/h (31 mph). On main roads: cars 80 km/h (50 mph), cars with trailers and motor cycles 70 km/h (43 mph).

Speed limits

Practical Information

	On motorways: cars 100 km/h (62 mph), cars with trailers and motor cycles 80 km/h (50 mph).
Safety helmets	Motor cyclists must wear a helmet at all times
Filling stations (Gas stations)	Near frontier points and on the principal roads these can be found every 20 to 50 km. Petrol can be obtained without coupons (Super 92 octane and Extra 98 octane). Diesel fuel can only be obtained with coupons which can be bought at frontier points. There is no repayment for coupons which may remain when the driver leaves Hungary.
Breakdown assistance	See entry

Travel Agents

Selection

IBUSZ
V, Felszabadulás tér 5, tel: 186–866

Budapest Tourist
V, Roosevelt tér 5–7, tel: 173–555

Co-optourist
V, Kossuth Lajos tér 13–15, tel: 116–683

Volán
VI, Lenin körút 96, tel: 323–171

Express (youth travel)
V, Szabadság tér 16, tel: 317–777

Duna
VI, Bajscy-Zsilinszky út 17, tel: 314–533

Travel Documents

Passport and visa	For entry to Hungary a valid passport is necessary. Citizens of non-socialist countries and stateless persons can only enter Hungary with a visa. Visas are obtainable, normally within 48 hours, from all Hungarian consulates abroad. A visa can also be obtained at a road frontier crossing point, at the airport and at the international shipping office in Budapest. Members of travel groups (spending four days or less in Hungary) who enter the country from Austria do not require a visa. Foreigners with a visa can remain up to the time stated on it (normally 30 days). A transit visa is valid for 48 hours.
Registration with police	Citizens of non-socialist countries must register within 24 hours of arrival or if they change their address in Hungry. Hotels, camp sites and accommodation offices will register for visitors and confirm this on the official document which is inspected by the Hungarian frontier police on departure from the country. Foreigners who stay in private houses must

register personally: in Budapest at the police station of the district in which they are staying, elsewhere at the appropriate regional, area or urban police station, the head of the family can register for everyone.

The visitor's permit can be extended 48 hours before time of expiry at the place of registration, at district police offices or at the relevant department of the Budapest police headquarters (VI, Népköztársaság útja 12). Loss of a passport, travel documents, visitor's permit or exit document must be notified immediately to the nearest police station. On the strength of the certificate issued new travel documents must be obtained from the appropriate consulate within three days, for which the relevant office of the Hungarian Ministry of the Interior (KEOKH, Budapest VI, Rudas László utca 45) will issue an exit permit.

Extension of visitor's permit

Anyone violating the registration regulations or exceeding the period stated on the visitor's permit is liable to a fine of up to 3,000 forints.

Violation of registration regulations

See: Currency Regulations
Customs Regulations
Frontier Crossing Points
Traffic Regulations

Useful Telephone Numbers

	Telephone
Emergency calls	
– First-Aid/Rescue Service	04
– Police	07
– Fire Brigade	05
– Breakdown Assistance	260–668
Information	
– Tourist Information TOURINFORM	179–800
– National Railways	429–150
– International Railways	224–052
– Long Distance Buses	182–122
– Air Travel	572–122
Foreign Office KEOKH	180–800
Automobile Club	
– Autoklub	260–668
Embassies and Consulates	
– Great Britain	165–858
– USA	124–224
– Canada	165–858
Air Lines	
– British Airways	183–299
– Pan Am	171–441
– Malév	184–333
Lost Property Offices	
– Central Lost Property Office	174–961
– Budapest Transport (BKV)	226–613
Taxi	222–222, 666–666
Telephone	
– Long-distance Calls (foreign languages)	172–200
– International Exchange	09
– Dialling Codes:	
To Great Britain	0044
To America and Canada	001

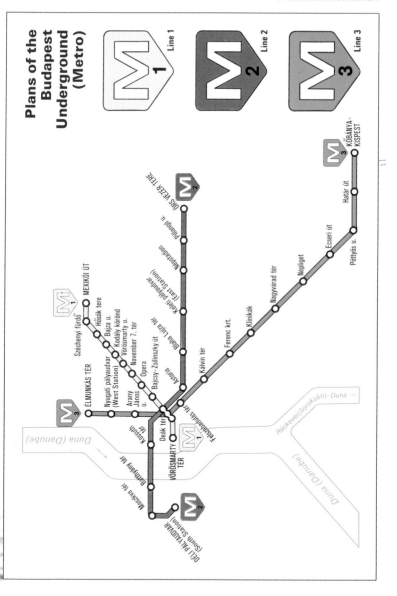

Plans of the Budapest Underground (Metro)

Notes

Notes

Notes